Cockpit to Cockpit

Cockpit to Cockpit

■ ■ ■

Your Ultimate Resource for Transition Gouge
Second Edition

Lt Col Marc Himelhoch, USAF (ret)

ISBN: 0692970657
ISBN 13: 9780692970652

Dedication

I WOULD LIKE to dedicate this book to my loving parents who instilled in me the values of education, discipline, and strong work ethic and then gave me the gentle nudge that provided the vector and momentum needed to forge a successful aviation career. I would also like to thank my amazing wife Missy for her loving support and motivation to see this project through from an idea to a reality. Without her strong business acumen, public relations expertise, encouragement, and love, none of this would have been possible. And of course, I owe a huge debt of gratitude to my book launch team, friends, family and co-workers for their numerous contributions to the success of *Cockpit to Cockpit*. Thank you all!

Contents

CHAPTER 1

Introduction

The Pilot Hiring Dam

THEY SAY, "TIMING is everything." In the airline industry, that is certainly a truism. In early 2014 I was staring retirement from the air force in the face. Sure, I could have stayed in past twenty years, but the airline-hiring scene was hot. The dam had finally started to break wide open; the airlines were starting to snatch up every military pilot they could get their hands on. In fact, they actually hired more pilots than they could train in a reasonable amount of time. This hiring overload was partially responsible for delaying my transition from military to airline pilot, although I could not have foreseen that in early 2014.

The dam I am referring to is the airline-pilot hiring slump that began shortly after September 11, 2001, and lasted for more than a decade, with the exception of a few years between 2005 and 2008. Pilot hiring between fall 2001 and fall 2013 was anemic, with only a handful of pilots being hired during that time. According to the US General Accounting Office (GAO),[1] the rate of pilot employment growth between the years 2000 and 2012 decreased by 12 percent. There were several reasons for this.

In the aftermath of the 9/11 terrorist attacks, demand for air travel dropped dramatically. In addition to the huge financial losses that the airlines suffered due to the terror events themselves coupled with the unprecedented Federal Aviation Administration (FAA) grounding of all civilian aircraft in the days that immediately followed 9/11, demand for air travel dropped by 30 percent[2] virtually overnight due to security concerns—not to mention the very real pain-

---

1 USA, GAO, "Aviation Workforce Current and Future Availability of Airline Pilots," last modified February 28, 2014, accessed April 3, 2015, http://www.gao.gov/products/GAO-14-232.

2 G. Logan, "The Effects of 9/11 on the Airline Industry," accessed March 23, 2015, http://traveltips.usatoday.com/effects-911-airline-industry-63890.html.

in-the-ass new passenger security procedures that popped up overnight after 9/11 and only got worse in the following years at airports all over the world. The airline industry saw an unprecedented furlough of pilots. Many airlines furloughed 20 percent[3] or more of their pilot force shortly after 9/11due to the reduced demand for air travel.

Another reason was the industry shift from three-pilot to two-pilot cockpits. The third pilot in many older airliners (like the B-727, L-1011, and DC-10) was called a flight engineer (FE). The FE sat sideways (behind the captain and first officer) in front of a confusing panel of switches and gauges. The FE's main job was to make sure the captain and first officer had plenty of food, coffee, and soda. The FE's secondary duties included monitoring aircraft systems, weight and balance, and so on. It didn't take airline management long to figure out that they could save a ton of money by phasing out three-pilot aircraft and replacing them with newer, more cost-efficient two-pilot aircraft. The majority of this happened in the late 1990s and early 2000s, compounding the pilot-hiring slump because, quite simply, the airlines no longer needed as many pilots.

Adding to the pilot-hiring slump problem was the FAA decision in 2007 to extend the mandatory airline pilot retirement age from sixty to sixty-five. That decision, probably more than any other factor, had the greatest impact on the slowdown in pilot hiring in the airline industry between 2005 and 2013. The airline industry as a whole was facing record numbers of mandatory retirements in the years following the 2007 FAA decision. The extension of the mandatory retirement age from sixty to sixty-five essentially allowed the airlines to kick the can down the road five more years.

Unfortunately, "five more years" happened to be 2010-2012, and the nation was caught in the worst economic slowdown since the Great Depression of the 1930s. The recession, along with a lack of capacity management (too many seats available compared to passenger demand) contributed to a series of airline bankruptcies and mergers that further delayed pilot hiring in the airline industry. By the time I retired in August 2014, the legacy carriers had consolidated to

3 J. Wynbrandt, *Flying High: How JetBlue Founder and CEO David Neeleman Beats the Competition* (John Wiley & Sons, 2004).

just three carriers (down from six just ten years prior). These factors drastically altered the pilot hiring landscape.

The first signs that the pilot hiring dam was about to break were the furlough recalls. Most US airlines began to recall their furloughed pilots in early 2013. By 2014, most airlines had recalled their entire list of furloughed pilots. The US airline industry is projected to lose up to 50 percent of its pilot workforce to mandatory retirements over the next ten years, increasing the demand for pilot hiring.

The writing was on the wall—the industry was about to face a record number of pilots reaching mandatory retirement age, passenger demand was at an all-time high (after the airlines restructured to return to profitability), and most airlines had exhausted their furlough-recall list. It didn't take a rocket scientist to figure out that the hiring wave was about to begin, and I wanted to ride that wave.

This was the status of the airline industry when I decided to retire from the air force in 2014. I had actually begun preparing for my transition to civilian life and a second career with the airlines about six months prior, in the summer of 2013. I knew my timing was good and the airlines would be hiring large numbers of pilots in the next few years. So why did I find it to be such an arduous process unlike anything I had experienced as an air force pilot?

As I began to research the process for transitioning from a career as a military pilot to a career with the airlines, I discovered that there was a ton of good information out there. The problem was that it was scattered all over the place. I discovered that some airlines use third-party websites for submitting applications, while others use their own company website. I found out about trip reports. I learned about airline hiring "windows"...you mean I can't just apply any time I want? Nope, you have to wait until they open the window. I found a variety of websites, books, and word-of-mouth about where and when to apply, what to put on my résumé, how to prepare my logbooks, where to find interview-preparation services, and so on. But I couldn't find any of it all in one convenient place!

That's where the idea for *Cockpit to Cockpit* was born. Being an anal-retentive, type-A personality pilot by trade, I decided to write a book of "How to

Transition from Military Pilot to Airline Pilot" to make it easy for future generations of all-American heroes like you. If you're reading this, chances are likely that you're a military pilot. As military pilots, we like to work with checklists. Consider this book your checklist for making the leap from military pilot to airline pilot. This checklist does not necessarily need to be performed in order. In fact, several steps will be accomplished simultaneously. The important thing is that by reading this book, you are educating yourself on the process, and knowledge is power. I hope to keep this book not only informative, but also fun reading for you. As military pilots, we have suffered through enough "death by PowerPoint" to last a lifetime. My goal is to write this from a military pilot's perspective…with all the sarcasm and sick humor that one would expect from a Friday pilot meeting in the squadron.

You might be asking yourself, "Why do you need to read a book about how to transition from military pilot to airline pilot?" Haven't military pilots been transitioning to the airlines since the airline industry began? Sure they have. But that doesn't mean we can't improve the process, right? I want you to learn from the mistakes of those who went before you. Isn't that what we do as military aviators? I want your transition to go smoother, with less pain; I want you feeling more prepared and more confident about your decision…and make no mistake about it; it's a huge decision for you and your family. You may not feel it now, but when the day comes (and it will) when you take off that active-duty uniform, it's a very scary feeling to not yet be hired at your next job. Just like playing on the monkey bars as a child, it's very uncomfortable to let go with one hand until the other hand has a solid grasp on the next bar. Reading this book will greatly increase your chances of stepping smoothly from one cockpit to the next (hence the title) in minimum time.

Everyone's circumstances are different but generally speaking, many military pilots will experience some financial stress in their transition. Pilots who retire from the military at least have their retirement pay to help them through, but even in that case you just had your monthly income cut in half. Unless you have done some serious saving (intended to be used for your transition), you will likely have some degree of "pucker factor" while waiting for that all-important interview invite.

Pilots who separate after their initial active duty service commitment but before retirement eligibility may feel it even more. It's a scary feeling to know your last active-duty paycheck is about to be delivered and you have not received a call yet from any airlines.

If you're planning to transition to the guard/reserve component, hopefully you can get hired by your new unit before you have to separate from active-duty. That provides some degree of financial cushion. But what if the timing doesn't work out? Now you have two job searches on your hands, an airline job search and a guard/reserve unit search. Talk about stressful huh?

Guard/reserve babies have a couple years of full-time to get some flying experience. Then the rug gets pulled out from under them as they become traditional part-timers and have to find a civilian job. Hopefully their unit can let them "trough" for a period of time while they seek gainful civilian employment, but there's no guarantee as those extra man-days are tied to the budget.

Any of the above can be a very stressful experience depending on your budget concerns and family situation. In the best case you'll be watching your savings dwindle. In the worst case, you'll have to go into "lock down" mode as you and your family seriously adjust your standard of living and discretionary spending.

Yes, the military to airline transition process can be a bit intimidating. I will equate stepping blindly into this process like going to the grocery store unprepared, with no grocery list, and trying to remember what you really need. Chances are you will spend more time and money at the store because you will have to wander up and down every aisle, looking at every item on the shelves to determine if it's something you need. Inevitably, you will come home and unpack your groceries only to discover that you forgot to buy some things you needed, and you bought duplicates of some items you already had. Admit it; you've done that! Maybe that describes your regular grocery routine (in which case you definitely need this book).

Now let's think about how that grocery run will change if we take the time to look in the refrigerator, freezer, and pantry ahead of time and make a list of only the items we need. We breeze through the store in minimum time—we know exactly what we need, so we only go down the aisles that contain those items. We also save money because we don't buy any items we don't need (except those damn Magnum ice-cream bars...those things are crack-cocaine addictive!). I think you get the point. It's always better to educate yourself about a process before undertaking a task...especially one as important as a career change (and this ain't no trip to the grocery store, I assure you)!

If something like this book had existed when I was transitioning out of the air force, my transition probably would have gone a whole lot smoother than it did. I'm trying to prevent you from making some of the same mistakes I made in hopes that ideally you won't even miss a paycheck between careers. In fact, I wish something like this book had existed from the very beginning of my career as a military pilot (shameless self-promotion: this book makes an excellent gift for any military pilot training graduate). Ideally, you will read this book at the beginning of your military flying career, because it contains some great information about things you can do from day one of your time in uniform to prepare yourself for a future flying career in the airlines, or any other flying job for that matter. But even if you weren't fortunate enough to have this book available to you that early, don't despair. It's never too late to apply the knowledge you gain in this book to your transition to an airline career—unless you're over age sixty-five, in which case you're screwed. But even then, there is a lot of talk (fueled by the impending pilot shortage in the 2020s) about the FAA extending mandatory airline retirement age to sixty-five or even seventy!

Let me be very upfront about what this book is, and perhaps more importantly what it is *not*. As I already mentioned, this book should serve as a checklist of sorts about how to make a successful transition from a military flying career to a flying career with the airlines (or other post-military flying job). I'm giving you the gouge (air force pilot vernacular), the pony, or whatever other term your service uses to describe a "cheat sheet." Now, I know that as military officers, we don't lie, steal, or cheat or tolerate blah, blah, blah. We do, however, as professional military pilots, learn from our own and others' mistakes and apply lessons learned to the next mission. If it helps you sleep at night, consider this book the "lessons learned" or "debrief focus point," as our Air Force Weapons School grads like to call it, that will allow you to succeed in your next mission...the mission of seamlessly transitioning from cockpit to cockpit (are you seeing a theme here?). This book will also give you some valuable information about topics related to getting hired at the airlines that most other sources don't talk about.

This book is not an airline interview-preparation course. There are several companies out there that specialize in airline interview preparation, and I will even recommend some of them in chapter 8. I don't want to compete with those services, nor could I...they are really good at what they do! This book is focused on the big-picture overall process of the transition from military pilot to airline pilot, of which interview preparation is only a small portion. Additionally, this book is not the only way to go about this process. There are lots of paths you can take and lots of advice available out there. The problem is, the advice that's out there is scattered all over the place. This book is designed to give you one resource with all the information, advice, and techniques you need, neatly packaged in one place. There was nothing out there similar to this book when I transitioned out of the air force...but I wish there had been.

Lastly, this book is not a guarantee that you will land your dream flying job right out of the chute (no pun intended for you fast movers). I will repeat this several times throughout the book, because I believe it's worth emphasizing: **Getting a job is a full-time job!** You will only be as successful as the work you put into it. It can be a humbling, frustrating process. Have faith! If you've worked hard in your military career, you're a decent stick (notice I didn't say God's gift to aviation), and you have a likeable personality...you should be able to get hired no problem, because the airlines love to hire military pilots.

Why the Airlines Love Military Pilots

As a military-trained pilot, among other amazing benefits, you get to move to the front of the line when it comes to getting hired at the airlines. I don't mean that in any way to offend our civilian pilot brethren. There are plenty of great civilian pilots (and plenty of lousy military pilots for that matter), but as a general rule, military pilots are a known quantity. Airline management know that military pilots get some of the best training available and are held to rigorously high standards. The same is true of some civilian training programs...but definitely not all. Military pilots also have very accurate military flying records of flight time and check ride performance, whereas civilian pilots vary in how well they have kept flying records, logbooks, and so on. Military pilots have to pass demanding emergency-procedures evaluations on a regular basis, usually in high-fidelity simulators. Again, some civilian flying schools can keep pace, but most cannot. So you can see why you have a leg up on the competition already, just having served as a military pilot.

But don't get too cocky; just because you're a military pilot doesn't mean you're automatically going to get hired. Remember that the airlines are hiring more than just great pilots; they are also looking for great people. I'm sure you've known more than one pilot in your military flying career who was an excellent stick, but also kind of an asshole (pardon my French) to you and others in your unit! Think about what the job of an airline pilot entails...spending just about every waking minute three feet away from another pilot for three to four days at a time. Do you really want to spend a four-day trip with that asshole? Neither do the pilots and human-resources (HR) folks who do the hiring at XYZ airline.

Sadly, I've known a few of these types who slipped through the airline screening process and are currently out there flying as airline pilots. I feel sorry for their crewmembers. The screening process is not perfect. However, for the most part, the airline hiring departments do a pretty good job of weeding out these prickly pears.

Much to the chagrin of your unit commanders, word travels fast in a flying unit when it comes to making the airline transition. You will quickly hear about it when others in your unit get called for an interview and get hired. I remember one prickly-pear pilot in my squadron who had an extremely negative attitude in general. He was applying to the airlines just like a lot of us. I had several conversations with him in which he expressed his disbelief that he had not received a call yet from any airlines. I wasn't surprised. Airline human-resources departments have screened literally thousands of résumés and applications...if you think they can't sniff out an attitude problem by looking at an application or résumé, then you're kidding yourself. It shows up in a lack of attention to detail and effort in your paperwork; I guarantee it. When my prickly-pear friend commented that "the process is too much work and not worth my time," it only confirmed my suspicions.

I'll return to my previous statement that **getting a job is a full-time job**, and you need to treat it as such. However, the payoff is worth the effort. There aren't too many jobs where you can make a healthy six-figure salary doing something you love (and would probably pay money to do... but don't tell that to management or the union), only work twelve to fifteen days a month on average, travel for free all over the world (and bring your family), and have the best corner-office window view in the world. Not to mention that when you land and shut down engines at the end of the day, there is no e-mail to check, no performance reports to write, no computer-based annual training requirement squares to fill...you get the point. But I don't need to sell you on being an airline pilot; if you're reading this book, chances are you've already made up your mind.

Consider This an Investment in Your Future

One thing you may not realize is that there is an initial upfront investment required when you choose to transition from the military to an airline career. The costs will vary, of course, but table 1 below shows a ballpark sample of what some of those costs are and how they can add up fast. I share this with you not to discourage you but rather to motivate you to take your job search seriously, because the quicker you get hired, the less it will cost you. Keep in mind these figures don't even include what it may cost you in terms of lost salary if your transition takes longer than expected between your last military paycheck and your first paycheck with the airlines.

The costs can be intimidating, but consider it an investment in your future. You are applying for a career in which you stand to make between two million to five million dollars depending on the airline and the amount of time you have before mandatory retirement at age sixty-five. I would say an initial investment of approximately ten thousand dollars is well worth it in the long run.

ITEM	COST
Airline application third party website membership fees (Airlineapps.com, Pilotcredentials.com, etc.)	$120
Interview suits (2)	$800
Interview-preparation course	$400
Travel (airfare/hotel/meals) associated with interview preparation course	$600
Travel (airfare/hotel/meals) associated with pilot recruiting event	$600
Professional interview attaché case/portfolio	$75
Electronic logbook software	$100
Electronic logbook binders/printer paper	$140
Professional application and résumé review service	$375
Professional job knowledge test preparation course	$300
Fees for mail order copies of records (transcripts, FAA records, etc.)	$45
FCC radio operator permit	$70
FAA class I medical	$80
Airline Transport Pilot-Certified Training Program	$4,800
ATP written test preparation course	$75
ATP practical training and checkride	$2,500
TOTAL COST	$11,080

Table 1. Typical Military to Airline Pilot Transition Costs

Don't let those numbers scare you too much. If you haven't already used your GI Bill to send your kids to college, you can use it to pay for the Airline Transport Pilot Certification Training Program (ATP-CTP) and practical check ride. You didn't really want your kids to get a good education anyway, did you? The costs shown in table 1 are typical of a military to airline pilot transition, of course everyone's journey will be slightly different. For instance, you might decide to skip the job fairs, or not use an interview preparation service to save some money. Just keep in mind that these services are designed to increase your chances of getting an interview and getting hired. After reading the remainder of this book, you should gain a better understanding of what career transition services are available to you, what each can offer to you, and how to find more information about them. Then you will be in a better position to make an educated decision as to which services you think you may need and which ones you can do without.

Getting back to my original point here, if you're going to invest that kind of money in your future, you probably want to invest the time and effort required and give it your all. The airlines love to see that "I'm fired up to have this opportunity" kind of spirit. They will recognize that you put forth your own funds and spent your own time to travel to that pilot recruitment event at XYZ airline, and that's what will separate you from the thousands of other applicants.

The remainder of this book will focus on a logical process for creating a successful transition from military aviator to airline pilot. Most of the information I present comes from personal experience. I was fortunate enough to have interviews with Delta, JetBlue, Southwest, and XOJET. Additionally, I received calls from United and Frontier, although I did not actually interview with either. The information I present was current at the time of writing this book; however, the airline industry is ever changing. Therefore, some of the information in this book may become out-of-date. I encourage you to contact me via the *Cockpit to Cockpit* website at www.cockpit2cockpit.com with any information you feel needs to be updated so that I can include current industry information in later revisions. The website also contains other products you may find useful in your transition such as practice tests, airline comparison spreadsheets, sample letters of recommendation, sample résumé, and so on. Some of these products are complimentary, others are included in the Cockpit to Cockpit Support Package for a modest fee.

Throughout this book, I will recommend many companies, websites, and books that you may find helpful for various phases of the transition process. A comprehensive list of these references and associated websites is located on our website www.cockpit2cockpit.com. I also want to emphasize that I do not receive any commission from any of the companies or websites mentioned in this book. If they are mentioned, it's because I think they are a good resource that you might find helpful in your military to airline pilot transition process.

As a retired air force pilot, I tend to lean toward air force terminology and process. I did my best to research other DoD branch equivalents to the air force terms and processes that I have referenced in this book. However, if you find any information in this book that is not applicable to the other services, or you have service-specific information you think should be included in this book, please call me out on it via the *Cockpit to Cockpit* website.

Summary

The airlines are currently trying to hire every military pilot they can get their hands on, and that outlook is forecast to remain valid well into the next decade. However, getting hired will still require a good amount of effort on your part because **getting a job is a full-time job**. This book is your flight plan to a smooth transition from military to airlines, in minimal time and with maximum efficiency. Be prepared for the upfront costs associated with career transition as demonstrated in table 1. Remember, this is an investment in your future! In chapter 2, we'll take a look at steps you can take, while still on active duty, to help prepare for a future airline transition.

The Checklist

As I alluded to earlier in this chapter, I want you to think of this book as your checklist for simplifying the transition process from military to airline pilot. To that end, I will include a checklist at the end of each chapter that will summarize the recommended action steps required of you to make a smooth transition from cockpit to cockpit. Since this chapter was just an introduction to the journey you are about to begin, there are no applicable checklist items, so we will start the end-of-chapter checklists in chapter 2.

CHAPTER 2

Preparing for the Afterlife

Exit Strategy

WHETHER YOU'RE CHRISTIAN, Jewish, Hindu, Muslim, or atheist, the fact is, there will be an afterlife...in this case defined as life after the military. If you are a person of faith, you most likely live your life in such a way that will allow you to make a successful transition to the religious afterlife. You go to your church, temple, mosque, or other place of worship on a fairly regular basis and try to live your life in accordance with the laws of your religion, all in the hopes of being accepted into your faith's version of heaven. That's called an exit strategy. You also have to have an exit strategy in order to make a successful transition from military to civilian life (the afterlife of the military). There are steps you can take throughout your time in uniform to set yourself up for success if your plan is to end up in an airline cockpit. Remember, those who fail to plan are planning to fail.

Let me be clear; I am not advocating that you make your transition to civilian life your highest priority while still in uniform. In the air force, we lived by the core values of:

1. Integrity
2. Service before self
3. Excellence in all we do

Placing your personal plan of becoming an airline captain ahead of your military service would be a clear violation of "service before self." Hopefully, you didn't join the military with the sole purpose of building flying time for the airlines. In fact, the airlines don't want pilots like that. They are looking to hire the pilot who lived by all three of the core values above (as well as some other qualities we'll discuss later). However, that doesn't mean that you can't do both...place your military service above your personal desires while still keeping an eye to the future.

You may also be fortunate enough to be reading this early in your military career and thinking that you don't need to worry about this stuff until you're within a couple years of getting out of the military. Don't believe it. There are so many things I learned in my airline transition at the end of my military career that I wish I had known from the day I graduated Undergraduate Pilot Training (UPT). Had I known these things back then, I certainly would have done some things differently from the beginning to make my transition easier in the end. The earlier you begin planning, the more likely you are to have a successful transition when the time comes. Even if you're not sure that you want an airline career after the military, much of the information contained in this book will still be applicable in allowing you to smoothly transition to civilian life no matter what career path you choose.

Probably the most important factor in your exit strategy is flying currency. Most airlines won't touch you if you haven't been actively flying in the past twelve months. Some are a little more lenient and accept applicants who have been "actively" flying two of the past five years (Southwest Airlines). They understand that staff assignments happen to the best of us military pilots. There is no magic number per se, but as a general rule, most airlines look for at least 200 flying hours per year. The better your twelve-month look back, the more competitive your application will be. Some airline legal departments require new-hire pilots to have a minimum of 100 flying hours in the past twelve months for liability reasons, but 200+ will keep you more competitive. Additionally, the type of aircraft and crew position you have been flying does make a difference. Obviously, Instructor Pilot (IP), Evaluator Pilot (EP), and Naval Air Training and Operating Procedures Standardization (NATOPS) flying time is much better than Second-in-Command (SIC) time. Additionally, multiengine jet time is more desirable than single-engine turboprop. General aviation single-engine flying is generally not considered currency by most airlines. Pilot in Command (PIC) time is best, however, the industry is changing all the time. As the pool of available, qualified pilots shrinks over the next several years, I would expect both FAA regulatory requirements and individual airline requirements to change as well. For instance, it wouldn't surprise me to see the airlines start accepting more SIC time to meet their requirements in the near future.

For active duty pilots looking at making an airline transition, keep flying currency in your cross-check as you think about when to make the decision to get out of active duty. If you know you are going to get out prior to a 20-year retirement, look for opportunities to do so while you're actively flying. If the threat of a non-flying assignment is in your future, perhaps leaving earlier rather than later might be in your best interest in order to get out with flying currency. The airline hiring wave should be increasing through the mid 2020s so earlier is also better for riding the airline seniority wave (read more about seniority in Chapter 4). However, if your flying hour totals and experience are too low and not yet competitive for a major airline then you might need to stay active duty until you build up some more flight time or transfer to a guard/reserve unit and accept a job with a regional airline until your flight times are more competitive.

For those of you who want to go the distance and join the "check of the month club" as military retirees, it becomes even more difficult to leave active duty with flying currency. As military pilots, we all know that the longer you stay in uniform, the harder it becomes to stay in the cockpit. Command billets that keep you flying are few and far between, and there aren't too many non-command flying jobs that keep you promotable. That means you might need to make some hard choices when it comes to requesting assignments later in your career. At some point you will probably be faced with the question: "Do I continue to pursue my military career, or is it time to start preparing for what's next?" There is no right or wrong answer. Ultimately it comes down to your individual situation and what's right for you and your family.

There are a few ways you can help yourself early in your career to get lined up for those elusive flying jobs later in your career. The best way is to excel in your flying community by progressing up the food chain as early as possible. You want to become a flight lead, aircraft commander (AC), IP, EP, NATOPS, and so on at the earliest opportunity. The more qualifications you hold in your weapons system, the more valuable you become to your service, and thus the more likely you are to stay in the cockpit.

You also want to get some "stink" on you. Notice I didn't say "odor"...I said "stink." As an example, you might want to get some "safety stink" on you by working in squadron/group/wing safety (read company/battalion/regiment for you army types or wing/group/fleet for you navy/marine types). By getting some "safety stink" on you early, you're more likely to be selected later in your career for a Higher Headquarters (HHQ) Safety staff assignment, which is generally an attached flying assignment. That means that although it is a staff assignment, it's one of those rare "flying staff assignments" where you will be attached to a flying unit to keep your flying currency because flying is considered essential for performing your staff duties. I used to think flying staff assignments were like the Yeti or the Unicorn...mythical creatures that are often talked about but don't really exist or you've only seen grainy photos. I became a true believer when I was selected for a flying staff at Twelfth Air Force Headquarters Standardization/Evaluation (Stan/Eval) as a numbered air force F-16 flight examiner in 2008. Although I was stationed at Twelfth Air Force Headquarters located at Davis-Monthan AFB in Tucson, Arizona, I was also attached to an F-16 flying squadron at Hill AFB in Ogden, Utah. During that assignment I was allowed to travel to Hill AFB one week per month to keep my flying currency. Stan/Eval, NATOPS, or your service equivalent is another good "stink" to get early in your career to set you up for a later assignment working a flying staff assignment at HHQ Stan/Eval or NATOPS.

Another surefire way to stay in the cockpit most, if not all, of your career is to become a Weapons School graduate (Naval Air War Fighting Development Center for US Navy/USMC). It is generally understood that graduates from these schools are among the best pilots in their service. Weapons School graduates, or "patch wearers," are sent back to their operational units to be the tactical experts. However, if you have a desire to be a patch wearer *and* an airline pilot later on down the road, I wouldn't say it too loudly in public. I think the Weapons School and their graduates generally frown upon those who desire to lead the cushy lifestyle of an airline pilot. They much prefer to keep you focused on turning our enemies into hair, teeth, and eyeballs on demand...which I think is reasonable.

Duty Titles Matter

In addition to safety, Stan/Eval, and aircraft qualifications, there are some key job titles that look very attractive on a résumé or airline application that you may want to strive for throughout your military career. Obviously, the airlines love to see the word "commander" in your duty titles. Having served as a commander shows that your branch of the armed services placed a high degree of trust and confidence in your leadership abilities. The airlines are always looking to hire pilots with strong leadership potential.

Another job title to strive for is director of operations (DO) or executive officer (XO). The DO or XO is directly responsible for executing the flying mission in a flying unit. He or she is usually the second-in-command below the unit commander. The airlines like to hire pilots who have served in this position because they know they are getting someone who understands the pressures of keeping a flying operation running smoothly, including scheduling, training, maintenance, and a myriad of other issues. The airlines equate this experience to being a chief pilot on the civilian side.

In the air force, we have a position called supervisor of flying (SOF) that also looks good on an airline application. I'm sure your service has an equivalent position. In the navy this position is called the air boss, and the air boss is the guy who likes to scream, "*I want some butts!*"...but that's just a navy thing (sorry, navy, I just couldn't resist the *Top Gun* reference). Anyway, the SOF, although not a qualified air traffic controller, works in the air traffic control tower. The SOF acts as a direct representative of the operations group commander (who is ultimately responsible for executing the flying mission on a base...usually an O-6 type). As such, the SOF is responsible for ensuring safe, efficient flying operations, including weather recalls, in-flight and ground emergencies, schedule conflicts, airfield status, and so on. The SOF has to be prepared to deal with any contingencies that may arise relating to the flying operation. In the air force, we joked that the best you could do as SOF was break even. If everything went normally during your SOF tour, then you wouldn't hear anything from the operations group commander…i.e. you broke even. However, it was very easy for something to go awry, in which case you were sure to hear about it…i.e. you lost. You can see why having a SOF qualification (or service equivalent) might look good to an airline looking to hire pilots who can handle stress.

There are also some temporary duties (TDYs) or temporary additional duties (TADs) you can apply for in the military that will help your case in the airline job search. Here's one that's often overlooked: US Air Force Advanced Instrument School (AIS). The AIS is a two-week course taught in Oklahoma City at the FAA headquarters. You air force types know that fun-filled Instrument Refresher Course (IRC) that you have to take every eighteen months as part of your instrument-proficiency check ride? As an AIS graduate, you will become qualified to teach IRC and, as such, be the instrument-flying guru in your squadron. In a fighter squadron, it's very easy to get sent to AIS, because nobody else wants it. Sure, it's not as cool as going TDY to Vegas for the Fighter Electronic Combat Officer Course (FECOC), but Delta Air Lines couldn't care less about a FECOC graduate. What they do care about is someone who is highly knowledgeable about instrument-approach procedures (some of my former weapons officers would roll over in their graves at that last statement, but even some patch wearers end up at the airlines).

Flying Hours

I think it goes without saying (but I will say it anyway) that flying hours are a key discriminator that airlines use to screen applications and résumés. No matter what impressive duty titles you rack up in your military career, at the end of the day, the airlines are hiring you to be a pilot. Therefore, they are looking to hire pilots whose flying hours in the military reflect their love of flying in general. The airlines are all about the bottom line. An airline doesn't make money with airplanes sitting on the ground, so it should come as no surprise that they want to hire pilots who fly for the pure joy of flying, not just to earn a paycheck. You have probably known that guy or gal in your squadron whose call sign was "Pigeon," because you practically had to throw rocks at them to get them to fly. The airlines don't want to hire pigeons; they want to hire eagles.

So how do you maximize your flying hours in the military? First, try to limit your nonflying assignments. I know; that's usually out of your control, right? We can't all be fortunate enough to stay in the cockpit our entire military career like me (don't hate me because I'm beautiful). Sometimes the long arm of the Air Force Personnel Center (AFPC), or your service equivalent of AFPC, yanks you out of the cockpit. If you see the writing on the wall, consider volunteering for the shortest nonflying assignment possible. In the air force, that usually meant volunteering for a remote ALO (air liaison officer) tour with the army. That would usually get you back in the cockpit in two years, and if you volunteered, AFPC would often let you choose your follow-on assignment.

We've already talked about the best way to ensure the maximum number of flying assignments in your career, and that is to upgrade quickly in your weapon system. Once you become an IP in your aircraft, you become very valuable to your flesh peddler at the Headquarters Personnel Center. Flying squadrons are usually short on experienced pilots. If you can upgrade to IP before you get yanked out of the cockpit for a nonflying assignment, chances are much higher that you will return to a flying assignment at the earliest opportunity, because the flesh peddler needs to send experienced pilots back to the flying units to keep the ratio of experienced-to-inexperienced pilots within the unit in proper balance.

On a more tactical level, there are some good ways to build your time in the air within each flying assignment. The first is to not get so buried in the queep of your secondary job that you forget about your primary job as a pilot. Queep is defined as anything that competes with your time and pulls you away from flying. It's easier said than done...Queepzilla is a formidable enemy. In recent years, pilots have been shackled with historic levels of additional duties, especially as military budgets shrink and the armed forces continue to downsize. That being said, if you neglect your additional duties too much, your evaluations and future jobs and assignments in the military may suffer, and that's not good either. Try to find a happy balance, and accept that it may make for some long days at the office. Keep in mind that you have the greatest job in the world...

you get paid to "slip the surly bonds of earth and dance the skies on laughter's silvered wings." That's a quote from the poem "High Flight," by John Gillespie Magee Jr. If you've never read "High Flight" you should be ashamed to call yourself a real pilot, stop what you're doing and go Google it.

Another highly effective trick I've found is to show up to work early and "hawk" the duty desk on those O'Dark thirty sortie briefings. More often than not, someone else will call in sick or oversleep, and they will need a pilot to fill in. There you will be...ready to go! If it doesn't work and you don't get to fly that day, tell your operations officer or executive officer that you want to sit in on the mission briefing anyway to prepare for your next upgrade. You can quickly become the rock-star young pilot in your unit this way!

Deployments are another great way to build flying time fast as well as building valuable combat time. The ops tempo down range is usually pretty intense, and you can rack up hours at a much faster rate than when you're at home station. Besides, it feels very satisfying to be doing the real-world mission and knowing you're doing your part for the war effort. You'll come home with some great war stories that work great at a bar on Friday night or in an airline interview when they ask, "So tell me about a time..." and you fire back with, "There I was, in the shit, inverted, air medals all up in my face, when all of a sudden..." You see where I'm going with this?

As a side note, try to volunteer for as many deployments as you can while you're young and single, because Mama (in the gender-neutral slang sense of the word) and the kids (in the time- and resource-sucking vampires sense of the word) won't like it if you repeatedly volunteer to leave them later down the road.

One thing to keep in mind when it comes to flying...not all flying hours are created equal. The airlines are interested in quality as well as quantity. As an exaggerated example: Pilot A has 4000 hours of mostly straight and level single-engine, Visual Meteorological Conditions (VMC) piston time. Pilot B has 2000 hours of multiengine jet time as an instructor, most of it at night or Instrument Meteorological Conditions (IMC), including five hundred combat hours. Guess who's getting the interview? As I said earlier, strive to upgrade as rapidly as possible in your weapon system. Currently, the airlines don't give too much credit for military SIC time. Military pilots who fly crew aircraft are put at a disadvantage by the airlines when it comes to flight times because of the way the airlines define PIC time for application purposes. You will see it clearly spelled out on their application websites. Most airlines don't use the FAA definition of PIC: time logged as "sole manipulator of the flight controls." The airlines consider PIC time as time logged as captain or aircraft commander, or the person who retains overall authority for the safety of the aircraft, which is quite different from "sole manipulator of the controls." As I said earlier, in the near future it may change, but for now most major airlines have a PIC time requirement so your SIC time won't count for much unless you meet the PIC minimums.

So how many flying hours do you need to get hired by the airlines? The answer is (you're not gonna like this)...it depends. Remember that they are scoring your entire application, not just your flying hours, to determine who gets an interview. Each airline's application website will post the minimum qualifications to apply. Usually the minimum is 1500 hours PIC time and an unrestricted Airline Transport Pilot (ATP) rating. Some airlines will also have minimums for multiengine, turbine, or other breakdowns of flight time. Even if you meet the minimums, you may not be competitive. However, other factors in your application can make up for lower flight times. For example, an applicant with 1800 hours total flight time and a master's degree, who graduated number one in every flight-training program in his military career, was an Air Mobility Command C-130 IP/FE, and has a B-737 type rating may have a higher application score than a fighter pilot with 3000 hours total flight time but none of those other qualifications (but I don't know too many 3000 hour wingmen...that's just a hypothetical example). As you can see, a strong application in other areas can make up for lower flight time, but if you have both, then your phone will be ringing off the hook as soon as you hit "send" on your applications!

So now you're probably saying, "Great, that didn't answer my question at all...how do I know if my flight times are competitive?" Patience, grasshopper! Here are some unscientific ballpark numbers of average military new-hire profiles I have seen lately:

2500+ hours total time
1500+ hours PIC
1500+ hours turbine/turbojet/jet
1000+ multiengine

Again, these are just rough estimates, and it all depends on the overall strength of your application package. The average profile of new hires will change over time as the industry fluctuates. Barring any unforeseen changes, the current projections show that the airlines will continue to hire at a historic pace for at least the next fifteen years. According to Boeing, the global commercial aviation industry will need 498,000 new pilots by 2032 due to retirements and new aircraft orders[4]. Nearly one-fifth of those pilots will be needed in North America. That means that the applicant pool will continue to shrink, and it will become harder for the airlines to find qualified candidates. As the applicant pool shrinks, the average new-hire profile will change also. Most likely, the airline industry will be forced to accept applicants with lower flight times in the future. If you want to see who is getting hired by which airlines and what kind of flight-time profiles they have, a good source is the pilot forums on www.airlinepilotcentral.com. Click the "Join the Forum" link in the upper right hand corner. You need to sign up for a membership, but it's free. Look for a thread called "Who's been hired?" Another great source is Ready, Set, Takeoff (RST). RST has a private Facebook group (you will need to submit a request to join) for each major airline (i.e. RST Delta, RST United, RST Southwest, etc). The RST Facebook groups are a great source of information and trip reports from those who have recently interviewed at the respective airlines. Read more about trip reports in Chapter 8.

Check Rides

In addition to your flight hours, most airlines will want to know about your check ride performance history, both military and civilian. From day one of your flying career, when it comes to taking a check ride, your "give a shit" factor should be off-the-charts high, because failed check rides can affect not only your military career, but also your ability to find a flying job after the military. That's not to say that the airlines won't hire you if you have one or more failed check rides. I know

4 "Help Wanted: Military Pilots to Fly Commercially," last modified June 9, 2014, accessed June 22, 2015, http://www.moaa.org/Content/Publications-and-Media/Features-and-Columns/Career-Features/Help-Wanted--Military-Pilots-to-Fly-Commercially.aspx.

plenty of pilots who had check ride failures at some point in their flying career and still got hired by the airlines. As a general rule, the airlines seem willing to give you a couple "freebies," especially on commonly busted check rides such as your Private Pilot License (PPL), Certified Flight Instructor (CFI), or UPT phase checks. They understand that things happen, and nobody is perfect. They are looking at the overall trend of your flying evaluation history.

However, with each check ride failure, your chances of getting an interview are reduced when compared with your applicant peers. There is also a big difference between a failed phase check in pilot training and a failed check ride after you have earned your wings. The latter become part of your permanent flying record. In the air force, they are called Form 8 check rides. Hopefully it happened earlier in your flying career rather than later. It's easy for the airlines to understand a check ride failure when you were a young, inexperienced pilot. It may be harder for them to understand a check ride failure when you're a 3000 hour IP!

Be prepared to explain your check ride failure circumstances both on the application and in the interview. Different airlines use different verbiage to ask this question on the application. Read the question carefully to determine if your circumstances meet the intent of the question. You may not need to list it on the application depending on how the question is asked, but you definitely don't want to lie! If in doubt, answer "Yes" and give a brief explanation in the remarks. Shown here is the verbiage used from two different airline applications:

> **Airline A:** Have you ever been removed from flight status, voluntarily or involuntarily, or failed flight training of any type, or failed any check ride?
>
> **Airline B:** Have you ever failed a flight check ride, proficiency check, flight evaluation, or upgrade attempt (aircraft or simulator)? Please include only check rides that occurred while attempting to achieve or maintain a qualification, i.e. instrument qualification, commercial, ATP, certified flight instructor (CFI), type qual etc. Do not include stage checks if part of a formal course of training or military flight training phase checks leading to your initial pilot qualification.

As an example, let's say you had a check ride failure in your initial military pilot training (not an uncommon scenario). Airline A is pretty clear-cut; you would have to answer "Yes." However, Airline B allows you to answer "No," because your check ride failure in this example was a military flight-training phase check. Let's say that based on the way the question is asked on the application, you determine that you do need to disclose your check ride failure. Most applications will give you a place to explain in the remarks. Here is an example of the right way and the wrong way to explain it:

> **Wrong:** Failed formation-phase check ride during Undergraduate Pilot Training T-6 phase.
> **Right:** Failed formation-phase check ride during Undergraduate Pilot Training T-6 phase. I have since passed every military and civilian check ride attempted, over twenty-five successful check rides.

Notice the difference? I turned the failure into a positive in the "right" response above. I didn't babble on about the details of the failure...they don't care if it was a bust for wing work or echelon turns. If I were the human-resources employee reviewing the "right" response above, I would be thinking two things:

1. It happened early in the pilot's training, and it looks like he went on to have a very successful military flying career.
2. We don't want him flying formation in a B-737 anyway.

Keep a Rope Handy

Here is another piece of helpful advice as you prepare for the afterlife. Keep a record of performance (ROP...pronounced "Rope"). A ROP is a file you keep on yourself that includes all your evaluations, training reports, decorations, training certificates, and so on. Even if you never transition to a civilian job (but chances are you will), keeping a ROP is a good practice in the military for several reasons.

First, when it comes time to write your promotion recommendation form (PRF), you will be glad you did, since every bullet you use will need to be justified from your records. You're probably thinking, "I don't need that; my commander writes my PRF, not me." In a perfect world, that would be true, but 99.9999999 percent of commanders will have you write the first draft. Do you think they have time to write PRFs on all the officers in their unit going before the promotion board each cycle?

Another good reason to keep a ROP is that any good commander worth his or her salt is going to ask for a copy of your ROP when you in-process to a new unit. You will impress the hell out of your new commander if you walk in to your first meeting and drop your ROP on his or her desk before he or she even asks for it...*boom*, you just scored a great first impression! Now you just have to keep from stepping on your proverbial schwantz for the next three years in that unit, and you're golden!

Some airlines (insert cough...Delta) will ask for this stuff when you show up for an interview. I think it's just part of the haze of getting hired at Delta to see how orderly you can present the mountain of paperwork they ask you to bring. Regardless, you can see there are many reasons for keeping a ROP, and you'll find it extremely useful throughout your military life and beyond.

Start a Journal of Stories

When you finally sit down for that airline interview that you worked so hard for, they are going to ask you a bunch of "Tell me about a time" (TMAAT) stories. If you're anything like me, you may have a hard time remembering stories from early on in your career, especially if you go the full twenty years or beyond. Hell, I have a hard time remembering what I had for breakfast yesterday, let alone a story from fifteen to twenty years ago. So I recommend you start keeping a TMAAT journal of stories that happen to you throughout your military career. The stories can be things that happened while flying or while performing your nonflying job on the ground. They can even be from before your military career. This is one of those "I wish somebody had told me to do this when I was going through pilot training" pieces of good advice that will definitely pay off in an interview.

As a general rule, you want to tell stories that make you look good. As a cardinal rule...*don't make $#@! up*. If there is no way to tell the story such that you come out smelling like a rose, use a different story. There are a few interview questions where it's OK to tell a story where you may have done something wrong, as long as it wasn't an intentional violation of the rules due to a lack of flight discipline (i.e., a crime) and there's a good lesson learned for you or the organization. As a matter of fact, in most interviews you will get a question like, "TMAAT you screwed up in the air and how you handled it."

Here is a list of the type of stories you should keep a journal-record of. This list is not all-inclusive but is a good cross section of the type of TMAAT questions you will see in an interview:

- ☐ In-flight emergencies: Note the details regarding weather, type of mission, good crew resource management (CRM) actions taken, and so on.
- ☐ Safety: Note what was unsafe and what you did about it.
- ☐ Conflict: Any story that paints you in a positive light regarding conflict resolution. It could be about conflict between you and a subordinate/peer/superior or how you dealt with a conflict between other crewmembers/coworkers. Hint: they like to see things handled at the lowest level.
- ☐ You had to break a rule or saw somebody break a rule and what you did about it.
- ☐ Leadership stories.
- ☐ Teamwork stories.
- ☐ Customer-service stories: In the military, the customer could be your student pilot if you're an IP, ground forces if you supported them from the air, the receiver if you fly air refuelers, and so on. Be creative.
- ☐ Empathy stories.
- ☐ Innovation, creativity, or improvisation stories.
- ☐ CRM stories (try to weave examples of CRM into all stories if you can).
- ☐ Training failures.

All the topics included in the list above are important qualities that the airlines are looking for in a pilot. Most of us can come up with enough stories to cover at least one story for each of the topics above. However, some airlines will really dig in on a particular topic that may be one of their core values. If they ask you three customer-service stories, will you have enough without having kept a journal throughout your career? Probably not.

Volunteer Opportunities

Volunteering your time and resources to a good cause is something that should come naturally. It feels great to help those in need, teach a kid about aviation, mentor a high-risk youth and see him or her get back on the right track, and so on. It's very easy to become so consumed in our own world, both at work and at home, that we forget the basic principal of "love thy neighbor" (not to be confused with "covet thy neighbor's wife"). Do your best to seek out and make time for volunteer opportunities throughout your military career.

Here are just a few suggestions of some of the more common places you can volunteer, but this list is by no means all-inclusive. Any good cause you believe in is a good place to volunteer. Habitat for Humanity, Red Cross, the Humane Society, Civil Air Patrol, the Order of Daedalians, Young Eagles, your local church or place of worship...the list goes on and on.

Volunteering also has a couple side benefits for a military pilot with hopes of becoming an airline pilot...it separates you from the pack. While you are still active duty, it will greatly increase your chances of garnering those quarterly and annual officer awards such as Company Grade Officer of the Quarter or Field Grade Officer of the Year. In the air force, individual award packages are submitted to an awards board. If the board has to decide between two officers who were virtually equal in their job performance, guess what? The award will almost always be given to the officer who has stronger volunteer activities.

The same concept applies when it comes to getting hired at the airlines. The HR folks will screen thousands of applications and résumés for each pilot position. The competition is fierce. Those volunteer activities may make all the difference in you getting hired instead of your peers. In my experience, it seems that volunteer work is especially important to American Airlines, Southwest Airlines, and JetBlue Airways. That doesn't mean the other airlines don't value volunteer work, but I have definitely heard from hiring officials with the aforementioned three airlines that volunteer work will help you get hired. Be prepared to discuss the details of any volunteer activities you list on your résumé or application in the interview.

Get an Advanced Degree

Trust me, I know how busy you are as an active duty (or guard/reserve) officer and pilot. However, I can't emphasize enough how important it is to knock out your masters degree as soon as possible. Not only will this help advance your military career when it comes to getting promoted beyond O-3, it will also increase your chances of getting hired at a major airline.

These days, airlines are looking to hire more than just good pilots. They value education and leadership just as much as stick and rudder skills. An advanced degree shows the airline that you have critical thinking skills, and the fortitude to persevere through tough programs (like airline training). It also shows that you may have potential for future management positions within the company.

An advanced degree is a huge differentiator between your résumé and the résumé of thousands of other pilots you're competing with for a job at the major airlines. When you attend a job fair or pilot recruiting event (I'll discuss more on those in chapter 7), you will have three to five minutes with the recruiter. He/she will quickly scan your résumé looking for certain desired items that separate you from the pack... an advanced degree is one of them. I distinctly remember meeting with a recruiter from a legacy airline and he circled my masters degree on my résumé. The rest of the discussion went well and I received a pre-interview call from that airline about a month later.

Advanced degrees are not cheap, however, as a military member you most likely qualify for the Post 9/11 GI Bill. The GI Bill should cover most, if not all, of the cost of your advanced degree, however it does comes with an increased active duty service commitment (ADSC) of two years from the date you finish your last class. The good news is that the new ADSC runs concurrent with your current commitment. In other words, if you currently owe four more years and you finish the degree in two years, you won't owe any additional time (i.e. your ADSC is still four years from now, not six years from now). Therefore, it behooves you to knock out your advanced degree earlier rather than later. Talk to your base education office for additional details.

Civilian FAA Flight Ratings

Even if you never intend to fly on the civilian or general aviation (GA) side, you will want to acquire as many FAA flight certificates and ratings as possible before applying to the airlines. Obviously, you will need to obtain an ATP to get hired (see next section), but it also looks good to get as many other certificates and ratings as possible that are not required. In short, it shows you are "well rounded" in terms of your flying experience and makes you look like more of a professional pilot. Some of those certificates and ratings include certified flight instructor instrument airplane (CFII), multi engine instructor (MEI), tail wheel endorsement, airplane single/multi engine sea (ASES/AMES), rotary, glider, and even balloon pilot.

Another good reason to seek as many certificates and ratings as possible is to add more points to your application. We will cover the airline computer-application scoring in more detail in chapter 6. For now, just know that filling out an airline application is much like getting promoted in the military...you want to check as many boxes as possible. As officers, we know that the chances of getting promoted without completing the appropriate level of professional military education (PME) and without holding certain key duty titles are pretty slim. The same principle applies when filling out an airline-pilot application. You have to check the right boxes.

The Aircraft Owners and Pilots Association (AOPA) and several other aviation groups had been lobbying the FAA to recognize the high standards that the military self-imposes on its pilot-training curriculum. They argued that graduates of military pilot-training programs should be awarded equivalent FAA pilot certificates and ratings without the need for civilian flight training. Finally, in

2009 the FAA updated the Code of Federal Regulations (CFR) and made it significantly easier for military pilots to get FAA pilot certificates and ratings via the Military Competency Test (MCT) system (14 CFR 61.73).

Now military pilots can simply pass a written test and show proof of military flight training to obtain a commercial certificate, instructor certificate, multi-engine rating, or instrument rating, from the FAA if they hold the equivalent military rating. That's right, no civilian flight training or check ride required. How cool is that? There are, however, a few caveats to be aware of. For instance, a military multi-engine fighter pilot can't earn an MEI using the military competency test, because the FAA will put a centerline-thrust restriction on your airplane multi-engine land (AMEL) rating. Therefore, you would need to go get a few hours of multi-engine instructor training and pass a check ride to get the centerline-thrust restriction removed. For specifics on the military competency tests, you'll want to read up on 14 CFR 61.73 and talk to your nearest flight school that offers the MCT.

There is a fantastic website that offers MCT preparation courses online called Sheppard Air (www.sheppardair.com). Their study method is simple, efficient, and designed to make sure you pass the test (note: not designed to master the subject material; see next paragraph). Just as this book is the "gouge" on the airline transition process, Sheppard Air's MCT-preparation service is the "gouge" on passing the test. They will even refund your money if you don't pass the MCT. I have used their service, and it works great.

A word of caution here: just because you're a military pilot and the FAA issues you a certificate or rating, that does not make you an expert in GA flying. GA can be very dangerous if you don't know what you're doing. According to the NTSB,[5] 94 percent of fatal aircraft accidents in the United States occurred in the GA sector in 2013. The 2013 percentage of fatal aviation accidents in GA is fairly representative of most years in recent history. In addition to risking your life, you also risk being cited by the FAA for an aircraft accident, incident, or CFR violation. That won't look good in an airline interview.

---

5 "Aviation: Data & Stats," last modified February 18, 2015, accessed September 12, 2015, http://www.ntsb.gov/investigations/data/Pages/AviationDataStats.aspx.

You will be required to get a flight checkout signed off in your logbook from a CFI in any aircraft you intend to rent or borrow. I recommend getting some additional instruction from an experienced GA instructor in the type of aircraft and type of flying you intend to do if you're planning to do anything other than day Visual Flight Rules (VFR) in the local area. For example, I was an air force instructor pilot in the T-37, T-6, and F-16 when I earned my CFII using the military competence test. However, I would never dream of taking on a civilian student and flight instructing on the GA side without first working with an experienced CFII to mentor me on differences between military and civilian flight instruction. I'm not telling you not to fly GA, but know your limits and get the proper training.

Obtain an Airline Transport Pilot Certificate

Prior to the passage of the Airline Safety and Federal Aviation Administration Extension Act of 2010, it was a lot easier and less expensive to obtain an ATP certificate. I was fortunate enough to sneak in under the old system. The new requirements took effect on August 1st, 2014. Those who were fortunate enough to have passed the ATP written exam prior to that date had two years from the date of their ATP written to pass the ATP practical check ride.

If you did not pass your ATP written exam prior to August 1st, 2014 then you must complete an ATP Certification Training Program (ATP-CTP). The average cost is about $4800. The CTP portion is now a prerequisite to taking the ATP written exam and the practical check ride. The CTP course requires 30 hours of ground school and ten hours of simulator instruction. Six of those ten hours must be in a Level C full-motion simulator representing a multi-engine, turbine aircraft and it must weigh greater than 40,000 pounds (the aircraft being simulated, not the simulator itself). To see the full list of requirements visit the FAA ATP-CTP website at www.faa.gov/pilots/training/atp. You can also look up the FAA approved list of ATP-CTP providers at www.faa.gov/pilots/training/atp/media/ATP_CTP_Providers.pdf

I have not personally attended a CTP course (as I said, I snuck in under the old requirements) but I have heard that military pilots will want to gouge their eyeballs out with a rusty spoon during CTP ground school. The FAA has mandated the curriculum and it covers in excruciating detail most of what you learned as a military pilot in the first six weeks of UPT. For instance, did you know that exceeding the critical angle of attack will cause an aircraft to stall? Yes, it's that bad.

The next step after completing the CTP course is to take your ATP written test. At this time, all FAA approved CTP courses are using Sheppard Air for their student's ATP written test preparation. It will be included as part of the course fee you pay for the ATP-CTP course. The ATP-CTP course is roughly a seven-day course and the ATP written is given on the last day. The Sheppard Air ATP written test preparation course requires 7-14 days of study preparation **PRIOR** to starting the ATP-CTP course. You won't have time to study for the ATP written during the ATP-CTP course because you will be too busy learning the simulator profiles and maneuvers, so plan accordingly.

The last step to obtaining your ATP certificate is to schedule and pass an ATP practical check ride in a multi-engine aircraft. You must pass your ATP check ride within 60 months (that's five years for the math impaired) of passing your ATP written exam. There are several flight schools around the country that offer ATP practical check ride preparation consisting of ground school and in-flight instruction. It typically takes about 4-6 hours of in-flight instruction (3-4 sorties) to prepare a military pilot to take the ATP practical check ride.

There are several good ATP schools throughout the country but as a military pilot there is one very unique ATP program you should consider, it's called MIL2ATP and it's located in Goldsboro, NC. MIL2ATP offers a course that includes a bundle of services you will likely need in your airline transition from some of the leading companies in the industry (I will discuss each of these companies in more detail in later sections of this book). The MIL2ATP airline transition program includes the ATP-CTP course from Delta Air Lines (think one week of training and schmoozing with instructors and hiring department personnel at the Delta Air Lines training center in Atlanta), ATP written test and test preparation from Sheppard Air, ATP flight training and practical check ride from MIL2ATP, application and résumé review from Checked and Set, interview preparation from Emerald Coast Interview Consulting, and most importantly (just kidding) a copy of Amazon.com best seller *Cockpit to Cockpit*. You will likely save yourself between $500 and $1000 total versus paying for each of these services a la carte. For more information visit www.mil2atp.com.

Other reputable ATP-CTP programs include Crew Pilot Training (www.crewpilottraining.com) and ATP Flight School, formerly known as Higher Power Aviation (www.atpflightschool.com). However, these companies don't offer the bundle of transition services offered by MIL2ATP.

It's probably worth mentioning that most regional air carriers will provide your ATP-CTP training for free as part of their airline-training program. If you're one of those pilots who might need to go to a regional airline to regain your flying currency and you don't have your ATP, then this path might be the ticket for you.

Summary

As you can see, there are a multitude of things you can do while still on active duty to help prepare yourself for a future airline transition. Flying currency and flying hours are just the tip of the iceberg. By starting early in your military career doing things such as keeping a journal of stories, focusing on duty titles, excelling in flying check rides, obtaining FAA flight ratings and certificates (including your ATP), and volunteering your time to worthy causes, you will greatly enhance your future airline application and résumé. Even though your time as a military pilot is limited due to the high ops tempo, if you can make time to get a masters degree your chances of getting hired at the airlines increase dramatically. If you wait until the last year of your time on active duty to start doing these things, you are putting yourself behind the power curve and increasing the difficulty of your transition process; but even if you are in the latter category, don't despair.

The rest of this book is focused specifically on the nuts and bolts of the transition process starting with how to prepare your logbooks. Even if you weren't fortunate enough to have this book early in your aviation career, if you follow the steps outlined in the remaining chapters, you should still be able to score interviews from your top airline choices and live the good-life of an airline pilot!

THE CHECKLIST

- **Strive to upgrade to the highest qualification in your assigned aircraft as early as possible.**
- **Pursue job titles early in your career that will lead to future flying assignments later in your career (safety, Stan/Eval, NATOPS, etc.).**
- **Maximize your flying hours using techniques provided.**
- **Strive for the best possible check ride scores throughout your aviation career (both military and civilian).**
- **Develop an exit strategy to ensure you have flying currency at the time you intend to apply to the airlines.**
- **Keep a ROP (record of performance) containing copies of all your evaluations, awards, and decorations.**
- **Be an active community leader; perform volunteer work.**
- **Keep a journal of flying and non-flying TMAAT (tell me about a time) stories.**
- **Obtain an ATP and as many other FAA flight ratings/endorsements as possible.**
- **Complete your advanced academic degree if possible.**

CHAPTER 3

Logbooks

LOGBOOKS ARE PROBABLY the most confusing and frustrating aspect of transitioning from the military to the airlines. I could have included logbooks as a subsection of chapter 2, but logbooks are a topic that warrants its own chapter.

As I started making my transition toward the end of my military flying career, I discovered that everything I knew about logging flight time in the air force was not applicable to the way the airlines wanted me to calculate my flight times. To make matters worse, I had about 300 hours of civilian flight time before entering the air force, and I needed to figure out if I wanted to combine my civilian and air force flying into one logbook or keep them separate. If I chose to keep them separate, how could I show my total flight times in various categories such as PIC, multi-engine, and cross- country, etc?

I was fortunate enough to have someone tell me way back in air force pilot training to keep my own logbook even though my flight time would be tracked by Air Force Aviation Resource Management (commonly referred to as "flight records"). That turned out to be a good piece of advice, since the air force flight records are not nearly detailed enough to fill out an airline application. Unfortunately I wasn't smart enough to use a civilian-style logbook. Instead I bought a military-style logbook at Army Air Force Exchange Services (AAFES). Here's a hint for you: using a military-style logbook is great if you're planning to fly for the military after you get out of the military (that was a weak attempt at humor), but if you want to fly for anyone else, you probably want a civilian-style logbook that will allow you to track all the categories of flight time the airlines are going to care about.

So there I was, one year away from retiring from the air force, with a civilian paper logbook for my GA flight hours, a military-style paper logbook for my military flight hours, and my official air force flight records. I knew that wasn't going to cut it for an airline interview, so I started asking for advice from some of the pilots I knew who had already interviewed and been hired at the airlines. That's when a friend of mine introduced me to the twenty-first century by showing me an electronic logbook. His flight records were meticulously printed on special customized logbook paper and placed in custom logbook binders. It looked just like a normal logbook except it was neatly printed instead of all the chicken- scratch, messy handwriting, Wite-Out, and mix of ink colors typical of a traditional logbook. I was sold! However, I quickly discovered that trying to merge civilian and military flying time into one neat electronic logbook was like trying to fit a square in the circle hole. It can be done with enough sheer brute force, but it ain't easy! Had I started using a civilian-style logbook (paper or electronic) from day one of my military flight training, it wouldn't have been so hard. I'll explain why in the remainder of this chapter.

Paper Logbooks

So which logbook is right for you? There are basically three different types of logbook you can use for an airline interview: the old-school paper logbook, printed reports from an electronic logbook, and military flight records. The only thing the airlines require is a copy of your military flight records (the whole thing, not just the summary reports). However, there are advantages and disadvantages to each type of logbook or flight record. Some people only bring military flight records for the interview. Others use a combination of military flight records and either paper or electronic logbooks. The next several paragraphs should help you develop a strategy for which logbook(s) is/are right for you.

The paper logbook used to be the only option in GA. When I was a private pilot student in the early 1990s (wow, I'm a dinosaur), my instructor would ask for my logbook after each session so he could sign it and log our maneuvers accomplished on that lesson, flight times, and so on. He would sign and list his CFI certificate number for each entry. Once I soloed, and after I earned my private pilot license (PPL), I became responsible for logging my own flight times in accordance with 14 CFR 61.51.

The paper logbook works perfectly fine and actually has some advantages over electronic logbooks. One of those advantages is that endorsements can be signed off directly in the paper logbook by your CFI and designated flight examiner. Endorsements are required for several reasons including solo and cross-country flight prior to becoming a licensed pilot. Endorsements are also required by the flight instructor who sends you to a check ride to prove that you have received the required flight and ground instruction for the certificate and rating you are attempting to obtain. The designated flight examiner will endorse your logbook to verify that you passed the check ride (hopefully). Some electronic logbooks also have a way to log endorsements, but the CFRs are vague on how "legal" it is.

Another advantage of the paper logbook is cost. You can pick up a good Jeppesen basic paper logbook for about $15. I recommend going with their professional version for about $30. With the professional version, you will be able to log more categories of flight time and track other currencies that will be important to the airlines.

Paper logbooks also have a couple disadvantages. The first is that it's very difficult to keep a paper logbook looking professional. Unless you are able to keep the same pen through your entire flying career (good luck with that), you will end up with a variety of ink colors. You will also fly with different flight instructors who will have different handwriting and different techniques on how to log your flight times and where they log certain information, sign, place endorsements, and so on. It's also very easy to make a math error when computing totals, and then you'll have to go back and make Wite-Out corrections that look like shit...except white. Do you really want to hand something that looks like shit to the airline interviewer as a representation of your professionalism? Another disadvantage to paper logbooks is that they can get lost or damaged with no way to backup the information.

Electronic Logbooks

If you are going to use a civilian logbook in addition to your military flight records, I highly recommend using an electronic logbook. The earlier you start using an electronic logbook the better. I say this because I waited until one-year prior to retiring from the air force to start using an electronic logbook. It took me the better part of three months to go line by line through my civilian logbook and military flight records and enter almost 3500 hours of flight time into an electronic logbook. I don't recommend this method, but in the end it was worth it, because when I sat down to fill out airline applications, it made calculating my flight times very simple.

If you don't want to waste months of your life entering thousands of flight hours by hand, there is now a company that can do it all for you called MilKEEP (www.milkeep.com). MilKEEP can take a scanned.PDF of your military flight records and create an electronic logbook as well as convert your military hours to a civilian logbook style. MilKEEP will provide you with a. CSV file of your military flight times that can easily be uploaded into any electronic logbook program you choose. I have not personally used the service, although I have read good reviews. If this company had been around when I was hand jamming my flight hours into an electronic logbook, I'm confident I would have paid for this time-saving service.

Electronic logbooks have several advantages over paper. We already discussed the extremely professional appearance of an electronic logbook. Most programs will allow you to print reports that look just like a paper logbook except they are typed uniformly throughout, as you can see in figure 1 below. Most programs also sell custom-made leather logbook binders (figure 2) to hold your printed logbook pages. They look just like a paper logbook but more professional. Here's another hint: if you have a lot of flight time (over 1500 hours), I recommend using the largest logbook style available. I didn't think about this until it was too late and ended up needing three logbook binders to hold all my printed logbook pages.

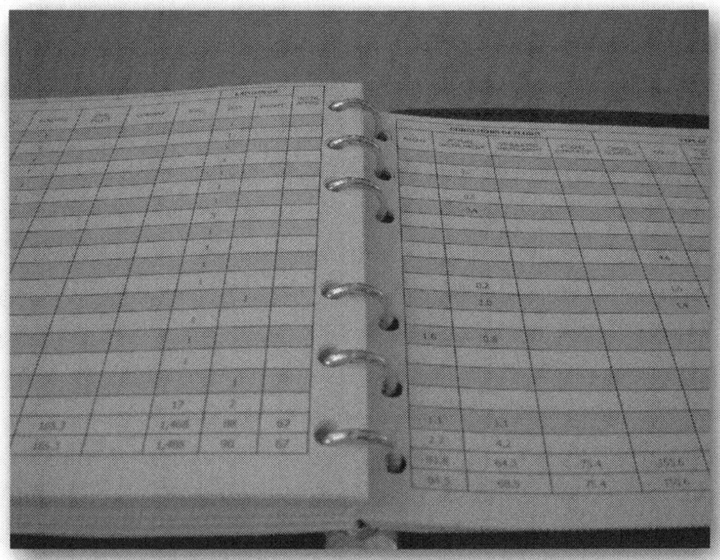

Figure 1. Printed electronic logbook page

Figure 2. Electronic logbook binder

If you stick with military flight records and paper logbooks only, you're going to spend hours totaling up various types of flight times manually when you fill out your airline applications, because the application will require flight times that the military and your logbook may not track. For example, Delta and United both use AirlineApps.com for their applications. On AirlineApps.com, the directions tell you to separate PIC time from IP time. However, Pilotcredentials.com (used by FedEx, American, and Southwest Airlines) directions have you include IP time in your PIC time. Some other examples I have seen on various applications that would be hard to determine using a standard logbook or military flight records include turbine PIC time, jet PIC time (not the same as turbine PIC time if you have any turboprop time), multiengine PIC time, multiengine turbine PIC time, and glass cockpit time.

It seems that every application website is different in terms of how they want your flight times broken out, but with an electronic logbook, it's very easy to get the information needed with just a few clicks. That's because electronic logbooks use pivot tables. Some of you über nerds know what a pivot table is, but for the rest of us Neanderthals, a pivot table allows you to filter information very easily from a database. Most electronic logbooks will allow you to filter by aircraft type and the type of flight time you are interested in. For example, if the application required night/turbine PIC time total: I could use the filters to select only turbine aircraft types and select only PIC time from the filters. Now when I look at the "Night" column, it will display exactly what I want: night/turbine PIC total time.

In addition to looking good and making it easy to tabulate flight times, electronic logbooks can track civilian instrument-currency requirements, FAA medical expiration dates, check ride expiration dates, and so on. Not only that, but they will warn you when your currencies are about to expire. As if all that wasn't cool enough, another benefit of the electronic logbook is that many programs are compatible with your mobile device. You can use your smartphone or tablet to log your flight time right after you're done flying, while it's fresh on your mind. Most programs keep your data backed up on "the cloud" (the cloud is a nebulous area somewhere between the stratosphere and the ionosphere that apparently is used to store electronic data), so you never have to worry about losing your logbook. In addition, many programs allow you to import your airline company schedule and will automatically calculate FAR 117 crew-rest requirements, per diem, and so on. As you can tell, I am a big fan of the electronic logbook.

The two electronic-logbook programs I have experience with are Logbook Pro (www.nc-software.com) and LogTen Pro (www.coradine.com). Logbook Pro is the program I used to prepare my logbooks for airline interviews. The program allowed me to customize the columns I wanted (and didn't want) displayed for my airline interviews. This is a very handy feature for military pilots because you can add columns to track sorties, combat time, night vision goggle (NVG) time, and so on.

Adding a custom column to track sorties was an especially handy feature while filling out airline applications because some airlines allow you to apply a military sortie conversion factor to your flight times. For instance, some airlines allow you to add .3 flight hours per military sortie (not per military flight hour, that's a common mistake many pilots make). If the application asks for your PIC time, using an electronic logbook you can easily use filters to show only flights that you logged PIC time and then look at the totals column for sorties and multiply that number by .3 to derive the military sortie conversion time allowed to be added to your raw PIC time.

The support provided by Logbook Pro is fantastic. Their website has tutorial videos, chat forums, and other resources. Additionally, when I had questions that I could not find the answer to, I was able to e-mail them, and they always responded in a timely manner. The only downside to Logbook Pro is that it's a Windows-based program and not Mac friendly. There is a way to run Windows programs on a Mac, but in my opinion it's complicated and not user-friendly. Logbook Pro Mobile is compatible with Apple devices such as iPhone and iPad, but the mobile version does not allow all the functions available on the desktop version.

The other program I have used is LogTen Pro. About the same time that I started flying with the airlines, I also made the jump from PC to Mac. After several unsuccessful attempts (admittedly probably caused by user error) to convert my Logbook Pro over to Mac, I made the conscious decision to switch to LogTen Pro. LogTen Pro is also a good program that has suited my needs, although I find it to be slightly less user-friendly than Logbook Pro. It has some great features including reports and integration with Airline Apps and Pilot Credentials websites (see chapter 6 for more information on where to apply). I have not tried to use their support services, so I can't compare them to NC Software in that category, although I have friends who love LogTen Pro.

For a more detailed comparison of many various electronic logbooks, there is a great article you should read on www.aviationbull.com titled *"Logbook Battle Royale"*. The author, Jason Depew, did an excellent job of comparing price, functionality, compatibility, etc. Jason also has some other great articles on his website about airline pay, and other related topics. Well worth a look when you have some time.

OK, so there are a couple negatives associated with electronic logbooks. They are more expensive than paper logbooks. Most services range from $70 to $100 for desktop download with additional annual fees for data-backup services and sync with mobile devices. In my opinion, the costs are well worth the convenience these programs deliver. Again, if you're an über nerd and know how to build a very complex pivot table, you might be able to build your own customized electronic logbook. However, if that's the case, then your talents are wasted as an airline pilot…you should probably go work for Microsoft or Google making a $350,000-plus annual salary.

Another downside of the electronic logbook is the ability to log endorsements. Some programs allow endorsements to be signed and logged electronically. Usually the field is locked once it's electronically logged, so in theory it can't be edited once logged. 14 CFR 61.51 does not specify how endorsements should be logged; it only covers the circumstances that require an endorsement. In other words, the CFR does not specifically address electronic endorsements. As a CFII, my technique if the student didn't have a paper logbook was to print the endorsement as a Word document, sign it, and make a copy for both the student and myself.

Military Flight Records

If you don't have any civilian flying time (or only a small amount that you don't mind excluding on your airline application) then you can just use your military flight records for your airline interview. The advantages here are simplicity and transparency. The airlines trust military flight records implicitly, and most likely you won't be asked to verify anything about your flight times in the interview. I know plenty of pilots who showed up to their major airline interview with only their military flight records and got hired with no problem.

However, you will get frustrated when filling out your airline applications, because many of the flight-time information categories required on the application are not tracked in your military flight records. I have heard of pilots making up rules of thumb to approximate certain flight times that weren't tracked in their military flight records. For instance, since cross-country time isn't tracked in military flight records, some pilots approximate 75 percent of their total flight time as cross-country time depending on the type of aircraft flown. If you use approximations, make sure you record the method you used to determine your flight times, and be prepared to explain it in an interview.

You will be required to bring your military flight records to the interview, even if you logged all your military flight time on your own in a civilian logbook. Don't just bring the two-to-five-page summary report; make sure you bring the entire flight records folder.

While I'm on the subject of military flight records, here is another piece of good advice: check your military flight records quarterly at a minimum and monthly if you can. Don't trust that the highly trained E-2 who works in flight records is going to keep your records 100 percent accurate. I didn't start paying much attention to my military flight records until I started transferring them to an electronic logbook toward the end of my air force career. Luckily, I had been keeping my own paper logbook (which is probably the only way you are ever going to catch errors in your military flight records), so I was able to catch many of the errors. I was missing combat time, missing entire flights, missing IP time, missing instrument time, and so on.

I'm not trying to knock the professionalism of our enlisted force. In their defense, they are responsible for keeping records on sometimes hundreds of pilots simultaneously and tracking many thousands of sorties, flight hours, and currencies annually. The error rate is actually quite low, but still it happens.

What I discovered when I tried to have my flight records corrected is that it practically takes an act of Congress to get flight records corrected from previous assignments. Therefore, it's best to catch errors while you are still assigned to that base, because once you leave an assignment, your records are shipped to a storage location in the basement of Area 51, which of course does not exist... in other words...man, they are gone!

How to Log Flight Time–Civilian vs. Military

If your purpose for keeping a personal logbook (paper or electronic) is to make your transition from military to airline pilot easier, then it makes sense to log your flight times in your personal logbook in accordance with the way airlines consider flight time on their applications.

As we discussed earlier, the airlines use a different definition of PIC than does the FAA. At the risk of being redundant, most airlines don't use the FAA definition of PIC: time logged as "sole manipulator of the flight controls." The airlines consider PIC time as time logged as captain or aircraft commander, or the person who retains overall authority for the safety of the aircraft, which is quite different from "sole manipulator of the controls."

If you fly a single-seat fighter like the F-16 or F-15C, then PIC time is a no-brainer...if you are the only one in the aircraft, then clearly you are the aircraft commander (AC), also known in civilian terms as the pilot in command (PIC). However, in trainers and crew aircraft, it gets more confusing. In trainers, if you are the IP, then any time you log with a student pilot or upgrading pilot who is not qualified in the aircraft is AC/PIC time even if the student was at the controls the whole sortie. However, if two IPs fly in a trainer together then AC/PIC time is not as clear. As a technique, always log the rank and name of whom you fly with in your logbook. If you are a higher rank than the other IP, then log the whole flight as PIC time regardless of what you logged in your military flight records for that sortie.

As an example, when I was a T-6A IP, if I flew with another IP, regardless of rank, we usually split the sortie time evenly between "primary" (time logged as the pilot actively flying the aircraft) and "IP" time on the military flight record for that sortie. So if we flew a 1.0 total time, I would log 0.5 primary and 0.5 IP. However, in my civilian logbook, if I was the higher rank between the two of us, then I logged the whole sortie as PIC. If I was the lower rank, then I didn't log any PIC time, just total flight time. If we were the same rank, then to be conservative, I didn't log PIC time either.

In the air force, we had an exception to this rule based on pilot experience level. If an "experienced" pilot and an "inexperienced" pilot (in accordance with aircraft-specific Air Force Instruction definitions) fly together, then the experienced pilot is considered the aircraft commander regardless of rank. In that case, if I was the "experienced" pilot, then I logged the whole flight as PIC time in my civilian logbook. Make sure you know your service-specific rules. These are just my techniques; you can develop your own. The important thing is you need to be able to justify your technique in an airline interview.

You might have heard that some airlines allow a conversion factor to be applied to military flight times. The reason they do this is because civilians log flight time from engine start to engine shutdown. Military pilots only log flight time from first takeoff to last land. Therefore, many airlines will allow a conversion factor to be added, usually .3 per military sortie (not per hour), to account for this difference in logging flight times between civilian and military. For this reason, I created a column in my electronic logbook to record the number of sorties for my military flights (sorties are also tracked in military flight records). In fighters, if we accomplished a training mission, air-refueled, and then accomplished another training mission, then we could log that as two sorties. Therefore, if using a .3 conversion factor, I could add .6 hours to that flight. The conversion factor can be applied not only to total flight time, but also to subcategories such as PIC, night, cross-country, turbine PIC, and total hours last twelve months.

Some airlines use different conversion factors, and some don't allow any conversion factor. When filling out airline applications, read the directions very carefully. For that reason, I don't recommend adding any conversion factor to your military sorties in your personal logbook. Keep your logbook as "raw" hours. Instead, I created a .3 conversion-factor spreadsheet that I used when filling out applications. My conversion factor spreadsheet is one of the many time-saving *Cockpit to Cockpit* support package products you will find available for a small fee on the *Cockpit to Cockpit* website www.cockpit2cockpit.com. As you will see, I am not a Microsoft Excel expert. You can probably improve on my spreadsheet or very easily create your own. I just want to offer you a time-saving alternative. No sense reinventing the wheel, right?

In addition to differences in logging PIC time and conversion factors, there are a few other tricky areas when logging military flight time in a civilian log-book. One of those is logging cross-country flight time (not tracked in military flight records). There are several definitions of cross-country flight time according to the CFRs, depending on what you are flying and the type of pilot rating you are using the time to achieve. The definition you probably should use is the 14 CFR 61.1 definition used to obtain an Airline Transport Pilot rating: time acquired during a flight that is a straight-line distance of more than 50 nautical miles (NM) from the original point of departure and that involves the use of dead reckoning, pilotage, electronic navigation aids, radio aids, or other navigation systems. Wow, that covers a lot of different scenarios, huh?

Here again, I have seen many pilots who just applied a rule of thumb to their military flight times. For instance, I know pilots who rationalized that approximately 75 percent of their missions took them more than 50NM from their departure point, and they used some kind of navigation aid or navigation technique during the sortie. Therefore, they just took 75 percent of their total military flight time and called it cross-country. I personally used a stricter definition and only logged cross-country time on flights that took me to another airfield (not just a military operating area or other military training airspace) more than fifty nautical miles away from my point of departure. Therefore, my cross-country time was just a few hundred hours. I still got calls from five different airlines including Delta and United, so I don't think it matters all that much. The airlines are smart enough to figure out that military pilots are highly trained in getting from point A to point B and know all the associated rules.

There is some bad poop floating around (no pun intended) out there in the military flying community about how to log certain flight times. Don't believe everything you hear. If in doubt, look it up. I have heard some military pilots say that all night flying time is also instrument time. Not true. Instrument time is defined as flight by sole reference to instruments. It is possible (and advisable) to fly on a clear night by using a composite cross-check inside and outside the cockpit. Use of NVGs definitely would not meet the definition of "sole reference to instruments," since you shouldn't be flying on NVGs in IMC anyway.

Simulated instrument time is another "gotcha" area when logging flight time. Both FAR (Federal Aviation Regulation) and military flight rules require the use of a safety pilot to help clear for traffic when practicing instrument flight in VMC conditions. Therefore, anytime I log simulated instrument time, I always note in my logbook remarks section the name of the safety pilot I was flying with. I have heard of military pilots being asked about this in airline interviews, and they had no clue about the requirement for a safety pilot. If you fly a crew aircraft, this one is no big deal, because it's standard operating procedure for the pilot monitoring (PM) to clear visually during practice instrument approaches. So how does this work for us single-seat fighter pilots? Technically we need a chase ship to clear for us when practicing instrument approaches in VMC. I'm sure all you single-seat, fast-mover types have been following the letter of the law on that one!

What about SIC time? Again, read the instructions carefully on each application website, as some airlines treat SIC differently than others. The FAA says you can log SIC time only in an aircraft that requires more than one crewmember per the aircraft certification. However, on the American Airlines application (www.aa.pilotcredentials.com) for instance, if you click the link for "Q & A," it explains that you may log student/dual time as SIC time.

Summary

As you can see, logbooks can be a little tricky for us military guys and gals making the leap of faith from military to commercial flying. Don't let it frustrate you too much. It's just part of the process. Remember, **getting a job is a full-time job**. The earlier you start keeping a civilian logbook, the easier it will be for you when it comes time to make your transition out of the armed forces into an airline job. Speaking of timing your transition, in chapter 4 we will discuss how and when to make your transition and some of the nuts and bolts involved in the process.

THE CHECKLIST

- Keep your own logbook (I highly recommend an electronic logbook) in addition to your military flight records.
- Log PIC time in accordance with the airline applications definition, not the FAA definition.
- Log times that are not tracked in your military flight records such as cross country time.
- Log aircraft sorties in addition to flight time.
- Research the FAA definitions for logging various flight times (Night, Instrument, Cross Country, SIC, etc).
- Check your military flight records against your civilian logbook quarterly to find errors in military flight records.

CHAPTER 4

Where to Begin?

Should I Stay or Should I Go?

ONE OF THE toughest decisions to make in a military pilot's career is the decision to either stay on active duty until retirement or to separate early to begin an airline career. If you decide to separate, that creates another subset of questions, the biggest of which is the decision to either join a guard/reserve unit part-time while working for an airline (and continue working toward a military retirement) or just be done with the military all-together and go full time airline pilot. I would love to layout some kind of "if-then" decision tree for you to help you navigate all the variables that could factor into these decisions but unfortunately I can't do that. There are too many variables that are unique to your situation and the decisions are highly personal. What I can do, is offer some things to think about when making these decisions and point you toward some helpful resources.

Most people tend to look at the financial bottom line when making these life-changing decisions. I would argue that while money is important, it should not be the deciding factor that leads you in either direction. Of course no matter what I tell you, you're still going to look at the dollars and "sense" of it (hahaha, very punny) so let me help you out. There is a great article you should read on www.aviationbull.com titled *"Military Pilot: Should I Give Up Retirement to Join the Airlines Now?"*. The author, Jason Depew (the same author of the article, *Logbook Battle Royale*, referenced in chapter 3) did an excellent job comparing the financial difference between retiring from active duty before joining the airlines or separating early and becoming an airline pilot. Granted, the article is a few years old and some of the financial considerations have changed including airline pay scales, military aviation incentive pay, and military pilot retention bonus amounts. Regardless, here's a spoiler alert; Jason and I agree...don't do it for the money.

Instead, my advice is to focus on personal job-satisfaction and quality of life for you and your family. In the realm of personal job-satisfaction, you should consider how very different being an airline pilot is from being a military pilot. Airline flying is never going to compare with military flying. It's hard to replace the sense of pride that comes with putting bombs on target, delivering critical war-fighting materials to the fight, gathering intelligence to help the battle-space commanders make the right decisions, providing air superiority, or air-refueling the aircraft that make all those missions possible.

You may also miss the squadron camaraderie and built-in social network of the military. That gets left behind when you take off the flight suit and go to the airlines. There are no roll calls, naming ceremonies, First Fridays, etc. The best you can hope for is a lively push to the hotel bar at the end of the day by the dozen or so crews that are staying at that hotel on any given night. The company does a couple functions a year for employees and families but it's not the same.

However, those perks of military life come with a price that we military pilots are all too familiar with: deployments, long hours, additional duties, and a seemingly never-ending supply of queep. As I think back on my air force career, it was about a 1:12 ratio as a conservative estimate. For every hour I spent flying, I spent about twelve hours busting my ass doing all sorts of non-flying work.

In my airline job I get paid to do one thing and one thing only, take paying passengers into the air and return them safely to the earth. If we can manage to do that and get them where they wanted to go on time with all their stuff intact, well that's just a bonus. The point is, I show up, I do my job, I go home (or to the hotel). That's it. There is no email to check at the end of the day, no queep, no performance reports to write. I know who the Chief pilot is but I never have to see him or her unless I've really screwed up (hasn't happened yet, knock on wood). You get the picture. This is truly a job you don't have to take home with you. My days off are fully mine to spend with my family or however I choose.

In the realm of quality of life, you should consider the seniority you give up by delaying a transition to the airlines. No more competing for promotions, in the airlines you get a pay raise every year until you reach the top of the pay scale. However, seniority has more to do with quality of life than pay. Higher seniority translates to better schedules, ability to use vacation weeks during high demand periods (summer, spring break, Thanksgiving and Christmas), choice of domicile locations, choice of aircraft to fly, earlier upgrade to Captain, and many other perks. In the airlines, you always want to be on the leading edge of a hiring wave. As we discussed in chapter 1, the current hiring wave is projected to crest in the mid 2020s.

Obviously, giving up a military retirement is a tough choice. A guaranteed paycheck for life with medical care is a very nice security blanket. For that reason, along with some of the reasons listed above, many pilots choose the trade-off of separating from active-duty and getting hired as a part-time guard/reserve pilot while starting an airline career. By doing so, they continue to work towards a military retirement. However, in this scenario under current rules, the retirement pay and benefits won't start until reaching age 62.

If you choose to go with the trade-off of both guard/reserve pilot and airline pilot, there are some other factors to consider. On the plus side, you get in early on the airline seniority. That is huge in terms of having the best airline career possible. You can also drop assigned airline flying when you have military commitments per The Uniformed Services Employment and Reemployment Rights Act (USERRA). However, don't abuse the privilege; that can get you in big trouble with your airline employer.

As with every choice, there are down sides to this one too. Having two jobs can be very demanding. One of the best parts of being an airline pilot is all the time off. However, if your time off is spent commuting between jobs and going to work at your other job, that leaves very little down time for you and your family. You can quickly burn yourself out trying to live that life. I'm not telling you not to do it, but I want to make you aware of all the factors involved. It can actually be a great option depending your personal situation.

If you decide to go this route, you want to make your logistical situation as simple as possible. The best possible solution is to get hired at a guard/reserve unit where you live and be able to drive to your airline domicile also. The next best choice is to live within driving distance of your airline domicile (or the job you will likely spend the most time at) but have to commute to your military unit. The worst possible situation is the double-commute, living in a different place and having to commute to both jobs. Avoid that situation if you can help it. Double commutes are tough, but sometimes we do what we have to do for family or professional reasons.

Finding a guard/reserve unit that's hiring and in the right location for you is not easy. Lucky for you there is a great resource to help you out called www.bogidope.com. Bogidope is a free resource that provides access to a fully interactive map of all guard/reserve flying units along with contact information and hiring notifications. The website also contains access to a wealth of informative articles on various topics related to transitioning from active duty to the guard/reserve component including early release from active duty programs such as Palace Chase, airline hiring, and airline pilot issues.

Choose the Airline That's Right for You

In my final air force assignment, one of my responsibilities was to match pilot-training students to their follow-on flying assignments in order to determine what type of aircraft they would fly in the air force. The students were allowed to fill out a "dream sheet" with their rank-ordered list of choices, which I would promptly throw in the trash and just pick assignments out of a hat...just kidding. I didn't take the job lightly; after all, I had their future in my hands.

About six weeks prior to each class graduation, I would sit down with the whole class for several hours and educate them about the different aircraft choices available. We would cover topics such as mission, career progression in that type of aircraft, base locations, deployment rates, and family life. I wanted them to have a firm understanding of the choices they were putting down on paper. Inevitably, in each class I would get one student who would ask, "So what's the best aircraft?" My reply would always be, "The one you get assigned to." The same axiom could be applied to choosing an airline.

At first, you'll just be happy to get a date to the prom. However, if you start getting multiple invites to the prom, then you can get picky. Even so, you still want to have a prioritized, well-researched airline dream sheet. Before we discuss the details of your airline dream sheet, I need to sidetrack to discuss a few important topics related to choosing an airline.

I guess this is as good a place as any to dispense with any rumors you may have heard about airline training contracts. When I was in your shoes, I had heard that airlines require you to sign a certain time frame (one year, two years, etc.) of commitment with their airline after completing initial training. The threat associated with those rumors was that if you quit before the end of the time commitment, you would have to pay back the aircraft type-rating training cost of anywhere between $20,000 and $50,000.

I can say with certainty that as of the time this book was written, the training-contract rumor is not true for the major airlines except Frontier. Almost all major airlines have no commitment at all, and you are free to walk away at any time. The only Part 121 (the CFR that applies to scheduled air-carrier service) major airline I know of that asks for a training commitment is Frontier. There may also be some regional carriers out there that have training commitments too, but I am not aware of them. When Frontier called me for an interview, they told me right up front that they have a one-year training commitment and asked if I would be willing to agree to that. I did not take the interview. That being said, I heavily researched and could not find a single instance in which someone actually was required to pay back his or her type-rating cost with Frontier (doesn't mean it's never happened).

Disclaimer: The information above regarding a lack of training commitment for various airlines could change in the future. However, even if the policy changes, they can't hold you to anything until you're actually hired and sign on the dotted line, right?

This Ain't the Military

Before I move on to discuss some of the comparison factors you might want to look at in your airline dream sheet, let me address the "all eggs in one basket" approach. It's simple...*don't do it.* Applying to only one or two airlines is a risky proposition. Your timing, the strength of your application, and the needs of the airline all have to match perfectly. Even if you were a Thunderbird, a Blue Angel, a patch wearer, a general officer…it doesn't matter. When it comes to applying to the airlines, there is no magic ticket that is guaranteed to get you hired. I have heard of several pilots from the aforementioned groups who didn't get hired for a variety of reasons. If you apply to only one or two airlines, be prepared to have a lengthy unemployment period if they don't call right away (or ever!) or you blow the interview and don't get hired (hey, it happens).

A better approach is what I call the "shotgun approach." Apply to all the airlines on your list that you would even consider working for. As previously stated, the major airlines are currently not requiring any training commitment. You can always start with one company and then trade up to a better airline if they call you later. Hold on to your hat, because what I'm about to say goes against everything we were ever taught as military officers.

The transition you are about to undertake is as much a mental paradigm shift as a physical change of job, aircraft, and location. As military officers, loyalty is a characteristic that is ingrained in our very DNA. Well, I hate to say it, but it's time for a blood transfusion.

I know that goes against our loyal military nature, but it's quite common in the aviation industry. Until you have multiple airline offers on the table, you should take the first offer that comes along. At least you will be employed and actively flying in the Part 121 world while you wait for another offer. In fact, if you get some Part 121 time, a new type rating, and more multiengine jet time under your belt by taking the first airline offer that comes along, you dramatically increase your chances of getting picked up by your airline of choice.

You are transitioning into the business world, a world where profit is the bottom line. They do not necessarily uphold the same high ideals and desirable personality traits that you and I were trained to value. This is an industry that has a long history of putting pilots out on the street if it means the company remains profitable. So don't feel bad about accepting a job offer with X knowing that you may walk away if Y calls. It happens all the time in the airline industry, and it's just the cost of doing business. You have to develop a survival instinct that says, "I will do what I need to do to take care of my family and put food on the table."

You have a highly desirable skill set. The airlines should, and will, compete for your talent. The airlines know that in order to attract the best talent, they need to offer a better deal than their competitors in terms of benefits and quality of life. That's the game, and right now the game is stacked in your favor.

OK, end of that sidetrack conversation and onto the next one. I need to give you a brief introduction to airline seniority as it relates to quality of life before we discuss your airline dream sheet factors so you will understand the world you're about to enter.

Airline 101

Here is a little airline 101 lesson before we discuss airline- comparison factors. Several of the factors listed in your airline-comparison analysis (see next section) are related to your "seniority." Seniority in the airline industry has a direct correlation to quality of life. Therefore, it is worth explaining how seniority works at an airline. Let's say, for instance, that an airline has 10,000 pilots and when you get hired you will be seniority number 10,001. The more pilots hired after you, and the more that retire or leave the company ahead of you, the higher your overall seniority grows.

There is also seniority relative to the other pilots in your same aircraft, seat, and domicile. As an example, let's say that you're a new-hire FO at Delta Air Lines. On day one of training, your class will choose their initial aircraft and domicile assignment. When it's your turn to choose, you have a choice between a B-717 domiciled at JFK airport in New York City or a B-767 domiciled in Atlanta. Let's take a look at how your seniority, and therefore your quality of life, will differ when it comes to your relative seniority to the other first officers in your aircraft and domicile.

In the choice above between a B-717 domiciled at JFK and a B-767 domiciled in Atlanta here are some factors to consider. The B-767 pays a higher hourly rate, but you will typically fly fewer hours each month. However, your relative seniority in the B-717 to JFK will grow much faster than in the B-767 to Atlanta because the majority of new hire initial assignments are to the B-717 at JFK. Why does that matter? The two main reasons are monthly schedule and upgrade time.

In terms of schedule, you will get off reserves and become a line- holder sooner in the B-717 to JFK. Being a line-holder means you have a known flying schedule for the month and you can trade your assigned trips with the company or other pilots. Think of reserves as sitting alert, something most of us have done in the military. You know which days of the month you're working, but you have no idea if, or where you will fly on those days. Typically you're on "short call" reserve of two-hour telephone standby (the time varies from one airline to the next). From the time the company calls you with a trip notification, you have two hours to get to the airport. That's not a very good quality of life. Sitting reserve from home isn't too bad if you happen to live within two hours of your domicile like I do (highly recommended if it works for you and your family).

However, imagine if you have to commute from where you live, to sit reserve for three to six days at a time in another city. That usually involves a "crash pad" (I didn't make that term up); an apartment shared with other pilots and/ or flight attendants. In a low-rent crash pad, there are usually multiple bunk beds in each bedroom available on a first-come-first-served basis. In a high-rent crash pad you can reserve your own bed; in theory nobody else sleeps in your bed when you're not there. Either way, it's not such a glamorous lifestyle huh?

In the example above, you might be a line-holder in the B-717 to JFK in just 6 months based on projected seniority increase, whereas it might take you up to two years before you can hold a line in the B-767 in Atlanta. Even as a line-holder, you still might need to spend a night in a hotel or crash pad on either end of each trip, depending on the start and end times of that trip, if you don't live within driving distance of your domicile. Now you can see why living in domicile greatly improves your quality of life

Your overall seniority also determines how soon you will be eligible to upgrade to other aircraft, other domiciles, and upgrade to captain. In our example above, the projected time for upgrade to captain in the B-717 at JFK is less than two years. The projected upgrade time to captain in the B-767 in Atlanta is over twelve years.

With each upgrade you need to consider what your relative seniority will be in your new aircraft, seat, or domicile. If you choose to upgrade to captain at the earliest opportunity, you will be the most junior captain at the most junior domicile...hence back on reserves with the lowest quality of life again. It's all about choices.

Your Airline "Dream Sheet"

As you get close (within two years) to getting out of the military, you will want to start doing some serious research on which airline is a good fit for you. I would consider what's most important to you in the next phase of your life and choose the company that best meets your needs.

Don't get so wrapped up in which company has the highest pay scale that you miss the overall big picture. Compensation is important, but think strategically about other long-range factors that could be equally important if not more important in the long run. I recommend creating a comparison spreadsheet to enable you to compare each airline side-by-side. Once you see the comparisons, you can then make an educated top-to-bottom wish list and start targeting your best options with appropriately weighted effort. I have created an airline-comparison spreadsheet, available for download from www.cockpit2cockpit.com as part of the *Cockpit to Cockpit* support package products. The spreadsheet uses a clever point system to allow you to properly weight the factors that are most important to you and your family and results in a score for each airline based on your subjective grading.

Before I discuss the individual factors, let me talk about some great sources for researching the most current information for airline comparison purposes. I highly recommend joining an electronic newsletter called Aero Crew News (www.aerocrewnews.com) produced by a company called Aero Crew Solutions, www.aerocrewsolutions.com. Aero Crew News is a monthly electronic publication that includes great articles and hiring information. Each newsletter includes what they call the Mainline Grid and the Regional Grid. The grids are tables that give a detailed comparisons of just about every airline's pay, benefits, fleet, domiciles locations, projected retirements, contract work rules, projected upgrade times, and other important factors.

Another great resource is a private Facebook group called The Pilot Network (TPN). As the name implies, TPN is a networking group for pilots looking to advance their aviation careers. Currently, TPN has over 15,000 members. Most are current or former military pilots like yourself and about one third of the members are current airline pilots. Therefore, it's a great place to ask specific questions you may have about a particular airline. Best of all, it's a free resource to you. They also have a great smart phone app (available for iPhone and Android) and a website, www.thepilotnetwork.org.

Now back to those airline-comparison factors. Obviously you will want to compare the pay scales. Not all airlines pay the same for flying the same equipment. However, something else you may want to compare that can make a big difference in long-term overall compensation is the upgrade time to captain. Most airlines have a very healthy pay increase when you move from the right seat to the left. If you can upgrade quicker with XYZ airline, that can make up for a lower pay scale.

Let's look at an example of direct annual-salary comparison for two generic airlines. For simplicity I assumed one thousand flying hours per year. I have removed the names of the airlines to protect the guilty and just to make the point that earlier upgrades can make up for a lower pay scale. From the data in table 2 below, you can see that both Airline A and Airline B fly the B-737. Airline A clearly has a higher pay scale than Airline B. At the time of this writing, Airline A's time to upgrade to captain in the B-737 is about seventeen years. At Airline B, the average upgrade time is ten years. For those not familiar with airline pay scales, it's worth explaining that most airline pay scales level off at year twelve. In other words, you make the same hourly pay from year twelve onward for your seat position (Captain or FO. The annual salaries shown below only include direct compensation based on one thousand flying hours per year. Also, a pilot who upgrades to captain enters the captain pay scale at the number of years with the company, not the number of years in the left seat. For example, a pilot who upgrades after six years enters the captain pay scale as a six-year captain, not a one-year captain.

Seat Position	Year	Airline A Annual Salary	Airline B Annual Salary
Captain	12	$235K	$216K
Captain	11	$233K	$214K
Captain	10	$231K	$212K
Captain	9	$229K	$209K
Captain	8	$227K	$207K
Captain	7	$225K	$205K
Captain	6	$224K	$202K
Captain	5	$222K	$200K
Captain	4	$220K	$198K
Captain	3	$218K	$195K
Captain	2	$216K	$193K
Captain	1	$215K	$191K
First Officer	12	$160K	$151K
First Officer	11	$159K	$150K
First Officer	10	$157K	$148K
First Officer	9	$155K	$144K
First Officer	8	$153K	$143K
First Officer	7	$150K	$139K
First Officer	6	$146K	$136K
First Officer	5	$142K	$130K
First Officer	4	$139K	$119K
First Officer	3	$136K	$107K
First Officer	2	$116K	$97K
First Officer	1	$77K	$57K

Table 2. Comparison of Generic Airline B-737 Pay Scales

Using only straight compensation to compare the two, Pilot A at Airline A would gross $2,490,000 total as a first officer for seventeen years; then, assuming a twenty-year career, he or she would gross $705,000 total as captain for the remaining three years. So Pilot A would earn $3,195,000 total over the course of a twenty-year flying career at Airline A.

Meanwhile, Pilot B at Airline B would gross $1,220,000 as a first officer for ten years; then, assuming a twenty-year career, he or she would gross $2,158,000 as captain for the remaining ten years. So pilot B would earn $3,378,000 total over the course of a twenty-year flying career at Airline B. As you can see, pilots make a shitload of money! But you can also see that earlier upgrade to captain can make up for a lower pay scale. Obviously, this example is overly simplified to make the point and does not factor in other benefits such as retirement plans, profit sharing, premium pay trips, and numerous other factors that can make a big difference when it comes to total compensation. Additionally, this example assumes that upgrade times are static, which is not the reality. Upgrade times at all airlines are expected to decrease as the retirement wave ramps up over the next ten years.

Speaking of retirement plans, another factor to throw into your comparison chart is what kind of retirement benefits are offered at each company. Higher 401K matching, profit sharing, and stock options can also make a big difference in the long run. Obviously you want a company that offers competitive benefits. A healthy 401K company contribution (often referred to as a B fund), when added to some profit sharing and/or a military retirement, can really add up over time!

It's also important to compare airline medical benefit plans and disability benefit plans for you and your family. Most major airline medical plans are pretty generous but the co-pays and premiums are usually a little higher than what your used to with military Tricare. Some pilots choose to keep Tricare as their primary provider but use their airline plan for dental and vision coverage. You can use TPN to ask pilots at various airlines any specifics about their company plans.

Short term disability (STD...no not that kind) and long term disability (LTD) plans are something most of us don't think much about but it can be hugely important if you ever need it. We all like to think we're invincible and we will keep our flying class one medical forever. I can't tell you how many airline pilots I've met who had an unexpected medical condition take them out of the cockpit for anywhere between a few months and few years. Luckily they had disability benefit plans to fall back on. When you're comparing airline benefits, make sure you look for disability benefits also.

Another often-overlooked airline comparison factor is work rules. These are protections built into the contract to protect your quality of life with respect to what kind of scheduling and pay shenanigans the company can abuse you with. Topics such as maximum number of days they can make you work per month, minimum pay for a trip, minimum block hours per month, commuting policy, maximum consecutive days on reserve, and a million other issues can really make your life miserable or fantastic depending on the contract work rules. The Aero Crew News Mainline Grid and TPN are both excellent sources of information to compare work rules.

Location is usually pretty high on most pilots' post-military priority lists. Of course, you're going to look at where each airline has their domiciles, but here are some factors to consider beyond just where you want to live. Which domiciles at each airline are considered junior, and which are senior? This will give you a good idea of where you will be located out of training and for how long. Certain aircraft and locations will allow you to advance in seniority faster than others. How long are you willing to sit on reserve at location X knowing you could be a line holder already at location Y? Are you willing to commute? How hard is it to commute from where you live to where you will likely be domiciled? There is a lot more information to be dealt with on this topic that could take up a whole other book. My advice to you is to talk to someone who works at each airline about the seniority picture in each aircraft/domicile and decide what's important to you.

Another factor to consider in terms of location is cost of living. What are housing costs like? Does that state have state taxes, and what are those tax rates? If you are retired military, find out if your retirement pay is taxed in that state.

When comparing airline choices, you may also want to compare your likelihood of getting hired at each. One factor that can strongly influence your ability to get hired is internal recommendations. You are far more likely to be hired at an airline where you have good friends and previous coworkers who can write you a good recommendation letter than an airline where you don't know anybody.

As we discussed in the previous section, seniority is everything in this industry. The number of new-hire pilots usually depends on two factors: projected retirements and organic growth (the number of new aircraft the airline is planning to purchase per year). Projected retirements are published in Aero Crew News grids mentioned above. The number of projected new hires at each airline for the next 12-24 months is pretty easy to find by asking around on TPN and you can gain some additional insight about organic growth by tracking aviation news about an airline's future fleet growth plans and aircraft purchases. When it comes to new hire numbers, the more suckers that walk in the door behind you, the better your life becomes.

You might want to compare the type of aircraft each company has in their fleet and the type of flying you want to do to make sure they are compatible. For example, if you envision yourself doing long-haul international routes, then you wouldn't want to fly for an airline that only has narrow-body, short to medium-haul aircraft and a mostly domestic route structure.

Leisure-travel benefits are also something to compare. There is nothing wrong with thinking about how you will travel the world on your time off; that's one of the major draws to the profession for most of us. Take a look at the cities and countries each company services. However, one thing you may not realize is that in most cases, your travel benefits for you, your immediate family, and your parents extend to other air carriers through a system called ZED (Zonal Employee Discount) fares. Most major airlines (US and international) participate in ZED, which is a series of bilateral agreements between air carriers that allow you and your family to travel space available on other airlines. For international travel using ZED fares, you only have to pay the taxes associated with the ticket. Taxes can range from fifty dollars to a few hundred dollars depending on the destination. That's still an amazing deal for international travel. Therefore, even if you prefer a domestic-only air carrier for work, you can still leisure travel internationally for free, or at least deeply discounted. Cool, huh?

One of the most important things to research is each company's core values and culture to see if it's a good fit for you. Some pilots prefer the pride and prestige that comes with flying for a legacy carrier, while others don't want to work for a company that big because they feel more like a number than a name. Just like the military, airlines go through good and bad leadership cycles also. I personally don't want to fly for an airline where there is an adversarial relationship between management and the labor force (maybe I chose the wrong profession, LOL). As you talk to your pilot friends at each airline, you will begin to get a sense of who seems happy at work and who doesn't. Try to get a good sample number of pilots from each airline, because there are some people who will always bitch no matter what the circumstances; that's just who they are. You don't want to form your opinion of a company based on one disgruntled hombre. However, if you start to see a trend of discontent from several pilots at the same company, that should tell you something.

Once you have your airline-comparison spreadsheet completely filled out, you can then rank order your choices from top to bottom. Somewhere in that rank order, you might decide based on your research that you would rather be a roofer in the hot Florida sun than work for some of your bottom choices. Draw a line, below which you are not willing to go there. Don't waste your time applying to any company below that line unless you just want the interview practice. In an ideal world, you would apply equal effort to getting hired at all the airlines above that line; however, this is not an ideal world, and your time is precious, so I recommend weighting your effort toward the top three. Now it's time to figure out when to take that leap of faith from military to civilian life.

Seven-Day Option and the Code 50 Extension

When you're planning your exit strategy, there are a couple tools you should become familiar with that you may need to help you execute your plan. Each service has their own rules associated with permanent change of station (PCS) assignments. The following discussion is pertinent to air force PCS rules but you can research your service rules to look for similar opportunities. Disclaimer: Don't trust what I'm about to tell you here as the gospel. The rules change all the time. Reference Air Force Instruction 36-2110, *Personnel Assignments* (or your service equivalent regulations) and contact your AFPC rated assignments manager (or your service equivalent position) for the most up to date information.

I remember the day in my air force career when I was first presented the option to turn down a PCS assignment. It caught me off guard. Up to that point in my career, when I received official notification of a PCS assignment I just signed the paperwork to get the ball rolling so the admin personnel could generate my orders. This time they gave me a choice, accept the assignment or exercise my seven-day option (often referred to as seven day opt).

The seven-day option is offered if you have less than two years remaining on your active duty service commitment (ADSC) when you receive PCS orders. In the air force, a PCS move adds a two-year ADSC, so they can't force you to move if the added two-year ADSC would take you past the expiration of your current ADSC. However, they can force you to get out. If you seven-day opt an assignment, you have seven days from notification of assignment to decline the assignment and establish a date of separation within six months. If you're in a flying assignment and looking to transition to the airlines with flying currency, the seven-day option may be something to consider.

If you are serving a CONUS assignment, the code 50 extension is another useful tool in the arsenal to help you separate or retire with flying currency. Let's say you are currently in a CONUS flying assignment and your projected Vulnerable Movers List (VML) will have you receiving PCS orders in June 2020 with two years and six months left on your ADSC (not eligible to separate until December 2022). In that scenario you would not be able to seven-day opt because the two year PCS commitment (June 2022) is less than your ADSC commitment (December 2022). You would have to accept the assignment.

However, anytime prior to the start of your projected VML, through your commander, you can request a one-year code 50 extension of your current assignment from the Air Force Personnel Center (AFPC) for pilot manning stability in the unit. If your unit is short manned on pilots (as they often are), then AFPC is likely to approve the request. In the scenario above, you would be able to stay at your current assignment until June 2021, but your ADSC remains December 2022. Now, if you receive PCS orders in June 2021, you are within two years of your ADSC. Since the PCS incurs a two-year ADSC commitment (until June 2023) that would take you beyond your current ADSC (December 2022), therefore you are now eligible to seven-day opt the assignment and establish a date of separation within six months (there is a provision to allow those officers between 19 and 20 years of total service to retire instead of being forced to separate).

Showing Your Cards

As I said in chapter 2, at some point you will probably be faced with the question: "Do I continue to pursue my military career, or is it time to start preparing for what's next?" There is no right or wrong answer. Ultimately it comes down to your individual situation and what's right for you and your family. When you do decide that it's time to start working on your transition to civilian life, you then face another decision...should you openly discuss your plans with your military leadership?

In an ideal world, all subordinates should be able to openly discuss their post-military plans with their leadership without fear of prejudice or reprisal. However, as I said a moment ago, this is not an ideal world, and there are some commanders out there who will punish you for "showing your cards" by giving you a lower stratification or otherwise less-than-fair performance appraisal, or assigning you to undesirable jobs, deployments, and follow-on assignments. I wish that weren't the case, and I certainly don't think it's the norm, but it does happen.

I was fortunate that my last commander was a great leader whom I felt very comfortable showing my cards. My commander knew I wanted to become a squadron commander. I worked hard to attain that goal; however, in my last assignment, it became apparent to me that although I was in the upper echelons of stratification among my peers, I wasn't one of the "shiny pennies" the air force was considering for command. The best I could hope for was a DO (second-in-command) position. I knew my commander was considering me for a DO position, but I had already decided that I was going to retire out of this assignment, so I showed my cards. I told him to give the DO job to someone who had a chance of making squadron commander.

I knew my commander well and respected him as a leader. He supported my transition to the airlines and even went so far as to write me a letter of recommendation. Not all commanders will be that supportive. Use your judgment and do what's right for you and your family.

If you are not comfortable showing your cards to your military leadership, The Pilot Network is another great resource you can use to get advice from current and former military pilots. You can use the private message feature of Facebook to keep communications confidential or reach out to other TPN members via the TPN App or website. For more information about TPN, see the "Networking Still Works" section in chapter 7 of this book

Unused Leave Time

As you get close to separating or retiring from the military, you may want to start saving your military leave time for the transition. You have three choices (or a combination of the three) of what you can do with your accumulated leave: you can use it as a well-deserved paid vacation, you can use it to go interview or start training with an airline, or you can sell back your unused leave for extra pay in your final paycheck. Which method you choose will depend on your personal situation. If you choose to use your remaining leave prior to your separation/retirement date, the military calls it "terminal leave." That always sounded kind of ominous to me...like I would be killed if I used it. You can also choose to use some of your terminal leave and sell back the rest.

Many pilots choose to use their terminal leave to start their transition to an airline job. This method works well if you can secure an interview (or several interviews) prior to your separation/retirement date. If your timing is really good, you might even be able to start training in your new airline job before your separation/retirement date. This situation is a huge moneymaker because you can "double dip." That is to say, you can use your terminal leave to get paid your normal military pay while getting paid by the airline from the time you start training.

If you don't have any calls from the airlines yet as your separation or retirement date approaches, you may choose to sell back your unused leave to get a bigger final paycheck. One thing you should be aware of if you choose this route...your leave is not worth as much when you sell it back. Leave that is sold back is only paid at your base salary rate and does not include "special pay." Special pay includes things like flight pay, housing allowance, and subsistence allowance. That can be a pretty big cut depending on how many years of service you attained before separating/retiring from active duty. Even so, it may still be the right decision for you if money is tight in your family budget and you're about to be unemployed for an undetermined amount of time...especially if you're separating instead of retiring and won't have that nice retirement check rolling in each month as a safety net.

If you are within two years of potentially retiring or separating from the military, you may want to consider "stocking up" on your leave balance by minimizing the use of unnecessary leave. It's nice to have a large leave balance during the transition to be used in any of the methods we discussed above.

Summary

For some people, the decision to stay in uniform or get out to start an airline career is a no-brainer. For others it's an agonizing decision that keeps them up at night. There are pros and cons to each path. You may also choose to live the best of both worlds by getting hired at a guard/reserve-flying unit while transitioning to an airline career. My advice is to look beyond the finances and think about what you really want in terms of long-term quality of life for you and your family. When you do make the decision to start your airline transition, don't forget to factor the seven-day opt and code 50 extension (or your branch of service equivalents) into your exit strategy.

Choosing an airline is an exciting, yet at the same time nerve-racking, process. Hopefully, the *Cockpit to Cockpit* airline-comparison spreadsheet will help you organize your thoughts and provide a logical framework for your decision. Again, the best advice I can give you is to think about more than just the money. Sure making more money is great, but not if your quality of life sucks as a result. Remember, in the airline industry seniority has a direct correlation to quality of life!

As you near the final last year or two of your time on active duty or full-time status as a guard/reserve baby, start stockpiling your unused leave time so you have a nice leave-balance to be used in your transition as either increased pay or well-deserved time off. Consider if you feel safe sharing your transition plans with your military leadership. If not, consider seeking confidential advice from current and former military pilots via The Pilot Network website www.thepilotnetwork.org or Facebook group.

THE CHECKLIST

- **Develop your transition plan. Consider the options (stay active duty until retirement, airlines only, or airlines and guard/reserve) in terms of quality of life and financial considerations.**
- **Research your seven day option and code 50 possibilities.**
- **Join The Pilot Network (TPN) Facebook group and website.**
- **Subscribe to Aero Crew News.**
- **Create an airline-comparison spreadsheet. Compare all the factors that are important to you and your family.**
- **Rank-order your airline choices.**
- **Decide if you are comfortable discussing your transition plans with your chain of command. If not, consider seeking confidential advice via The Pilot Network.**
- **Develop an "unused leave" strategy.**

CHAPTER 5

Paperwork

THERE IS A lot of paperwork required when applying to be an airline pilot. Some of it you will need for your application, some for the interview, and some for both. I recommend you start gathering as much of the required and recommended paperwork as possible before beginning your applications. However, don't miss an opened airline application window just because you're waiting on some paperwork. Most applications will allow you to submit and then go back and update later.

Not everything in this chapter will be required by all airlines, but it's a good idea to gather everything in this chapter ahead of time anyway. Some airlines give very short lead time for interview notification. I have seen as little as one week's notice! The week before your interview is not the time to send out requests to government agencies for paperwork...you work in the government, and you know how slow they can be!

Transcripts

Some airlines will require official college and high-school transcripts. Usually they won't be required on the application, but they may be required at the interview. However, even if they don't ask you to upload the transcripts with the application, they will very likely ask you for your grade-point average (GPA). Unless you can remember your high-school and college GPAs, you will need a copy of your transcripts.

I recommend ordering several (three to five) copies of each transcript. You will probably interview with more than one airline. Remember that "official" transcripts need to remain sealed in the envelope they were mailed in. I ordered five official copies of both my high-school and college transcripts. I opened one of each (making them unofficial) so I could get my GPA for my applications, and I left the others sealed for interviews.

Flight Evaluation Folder

Since you are applying for a professional pilot job, the airline will most likely want to see your performance on your civilian and military check rides. This paragraph is specific to only your military check-ride records. In the air force, it's called your flight evaluation folder (FEF). The FEF contains all your Form 8s from every check ride you took as a rated pilot in the military. Other DoD branches may use different terminology and form numbers, but the concept is universal; you will need to bring documentation of your performance on all your military check rides.

Make sure you bring the whole folder containing each individual Form 8, not just the summary page showing your overall grade on each check ride. If you are still in the military when you have your airline interview, you will probably need to photocopy your entire FEF and bring the copies with you. I can speak for the air force, and I suspect the other DoD services are the same, when I say that they don't like you taking your FEF out of the office for any reason until you separate or retire.

Flight Records

Almost all the caveats above for FEFs also apply to your flight records. Your flight records will have the breakdown and summary of all your military flying time. Your flight records (along with civilian logbooks) are used to verify the flight times you listed on your application. Make sure they match. If there are differences, be prepared to explain in the interview.

Again, make sure you bring the whole folder that includes all individual sorties flown, not just the summary reports. The summary reports are usually handy for filling out your applications, but they won't have all the flight times required by the application, as was discussed in chapter 3. Here again, you will probably need to bring copies instead of the real flight records if you are still in the military.

Logbooks

You will definitely need your logbooks when filling out applications and for the interview. This is where that electronic logbook really comes in handy. If you are only using military flight time, then you may choose to only use your military flight records for the interview. However, you will need to be able to explain in an interview how you calculated any flight times listed on your application that are not tracked by your military flight records.

If you have kept a paper logbook, go through it with a fine-tooth comb and make sure all entries are complete, each page is signed, all endorsements are included, and the flight times and totals are accurate.

If you used an electronic logbook, you will probably want to print it in standard paper-logbook format. Your software company should sell logbook printer paper and binders compatible with your software on their website. *Do not wait until the last minute to print your logbook!* Printing the logbook for the first time can be a very time-consuming, frustrating process. It will probably take you several attempts and phone calls to the software-company support line to get it right (see chapter 3, "Electronic Logbooks"). However, once you get it printed correctly, it will look great, and you will walk into your airline interview with the confidence of knowing you have the best-looking logbooks in the bunch!

Passport

You need one...make sure it's current. If you don't have a passport or need to renew a passport, go to the State Department travel website: www.travel.state.gov/content/passports/en/passports/apply.html. You may also use the link located on www.cockpit2cockpit.com. It can take several months to process a passport application, so make sure you lead turn this one. There are services available that can get you a passport in a matter of days, but the less time you have, the more you get screwed on the price, so plan ahead if you want to avoid spending several hundred dollars.

Driving Records

Airlineapplications.com (used by Delta and United) will ask you to list details of all driving infractions, including tickets and accidents, on the application. Additionally, some airlines will ask you to bring a copy of your driving records to the interview. Therefore, you will need to obtain a copy of your driving records. There are two different driving records I recommend obtaining.

The first is called the National Driver's Registry (NDR). The NDR lists all drivers who have ever received a DUI or DWI or had their license suspended or revoked. Now you may be thinking, "Great, none of those has ever happened to me, so I don't need a copy of my NDR search." Not so fast. It is rare, but it has happened that people's names or driver's license numbers have ended up on the NDR by accident because some knucklehead at the Department of Motor Vehicles typed the wrong driver's license number into the computer. Say it isn't so?

I'll bet you would sure like to clear that up before your interview rather than find out about the mistake during your interview, huh? For instructions on how to obtain a clearance letter from the National Highway Traffic Safety Administration showing that a search of your driving record was completed and you're not on the naughty list, go to www.one.nhtsa.gov/Data/National-Driver-Register-(NDR). Look for the "frequently asked questions" link. You may also use the link located on www.cockpit2cockpit.com.

The other driving records you will want to obtain are those from each state in which you have been issued a driver's license. These records will list the details of any tickets, violations, and so on. You can use these records to fill in the blanks on your application regarding driving infractions. The source for these records varies widely from state to state, but a quick Google search ought to point you in the right direction without too much difficulty.

By the way, just because an airline application doesn't ask for your driving-record details or they don't ask you to bring a copy, does not mean that they won't conduct a search on their own. Read the fine print on what you are agreeing to when you sign the application before you hit submit. Basically, you have given them permission to dig into just about anything from your past that they want to.

FCC Radiotelephone Operator's Permit

Each airline application website will list the minimum requirements for getting hired as a pilot with that company. Most will require that you obtain an FCC Radiotelephone Operator's Permit. You may see this referred to in various places as a ROP, an RP, an RR, or a Restricted Radiotelephone Operator's Permit. They are all the same thing, and acquiring one is quite simple.

In my opinion, this permit is just a way for the FCC to extort $70 from you, because all you need to get one is to fill out an application and send $70 to the FCC. In other words, they will give one to anybody who pays. However, it is a requirement to have a ROP when talking on an aircraft's radio outside the United States. Since most airlines will require you to get it and will ask on the application if you have one, I guess you better fork over that $70 bucks. To get your ROP or RR or $70 piece of paper, or whatever you want to call it…just go to this website and follow the directions: www.wireless.fcc.gov/commoperators/index.htm?job=rr. You may also use the link located on www.cockpit2cockpit.com. Of course, in standard government fashion, they make it ridiculously complicated to find the actual payment amount and method (It's contained in a separate document called *FCC Wireless Telecommunications Bureau Fee Filing Guide*).

FAA First Class Medical

You will need to acquire (and keep current) an FAA First Class Medical. FAA medicals are much easier to pass than military Flying Class 1 physicals, so if you had no problems staying on flying status in the military, you should have no issues obtaining an FAA First Class Medical. Every airline will ask for it both on the application and in the interview. If you are under age forty, then a First Class Medical is good for a year for ATP privileges. If you're over age forty, then it's only good for six months and includes an electrocardiogram (EKG) every other renewal period. An FAA First Class Medical costs about $80 (add another $80 if you are having the EKG done with it).

Some military flight docs are qualified as FAA Aviation Medical Examiners (AMEs). If your flight doc is also an AME, then you can kill two birds with one stone and ask him or her to do the First Class Medical as part of your annual military flight physical. If your flight doc is not an AME, you can use this website to find your nearest AME: www.faa.gov/pilots/ame-locator. You may also use the link located on www.cockpit2cockpit.com.

You will need to create an account on FAA Med Express at their website: www.medxpress.faa.gov. Before your appointment, go to the website and fill out a Form 8500 Application for Airmen Medical. Print a copy and bring it with you to your appointment.

A quick sidebar about FAA medicals and VA Disability: since you will be leaving military service, it's very likely that you will be applying for VA disability benefits...and you should. More than likely you have some service-connected ailments, and you have earned the associated VA benefits. It is possible, and quite common, to be on VA disability and hold an FAA First Class Medical; there is no disqualifying VA disability percentage with respect to obtaining an FAA First Class Medical. Each medical condition will be evaluated on its own merit.

When you apply for, or renew, an FAA First Class Medical, you will be asked to disclose any medical issues for which you are receiving disability benefits. Your AME may ask you about those disability medical conditions. He or she may also require a doctor's note to say that the problem will not affect your ability to fly.

While I'm already on the VA disability sidebar, I'll give you another helpful piece of advice. No matter what anyone tells you, don't wait until after you are officially separated or retired to submit your initial disability claim. Submit it while you are still on active duty. I got some bad advice from my VA assistance representative, and hence it took twice as long to get my claim processed. If you submit your claim while still on active duty (or still in the Reserves or National Guard), your claim goes to the front of the VA line. If you wait until you separate or retire, your claim goes to the back of the line with the hundreds of thousands of other VA claims from veterans dating back as far as World War II! I'm not saying those guys don't deserve to be in line ahead of you, because they do.

FAA Airman's Medical and Flying Records

When you score an interview, the airline will ask you to fill out Pilot Record's Improvement Act (PRIA) paperwork. One of these forms, PRIA Form 8060-10, gives your consent to the airline to receive a copy of all your FAA medical and pilot records.

Wouldn't it be nice if you could obtain a copy of those records before the airline sees them in case there are any mix-ups that need to be cleared up? Well, you're in luck. You can request a copy of all your FAA medical and pilot records by visiting the FAA website at www.faa.gov/licenses_certificates/airmen_certification. You may also use the link located on www.cockpit2cockpit.com.

They will give you instructions for requesting your records. It costs about $25, but that's well worth the peace of mind knowing there are no "show stoppers" in your records.

Letters of Recommendation

It is very important to get some letters of recommendation (LORs) for each airline that you apply to. Some airlines are bigger on this than others in terms of how many letters you need. There is no magic number, but in general I would say to strive for three to five LORs for each company you apply to. In general, internal recommendations (from those within the company) count for more points than external recommendations. They don't all have to be internal LORs, but the more the better.

You want to be sure the person you are asking to write you a recommendation is somebody whose reputation is in good standing with the company. For instance, if you know a pilot is difficult to get along with, you might not want a recommendation letter from that person. It could actually hurt your chances of getting hired, because he or she may have pissed off some of the folks in the hiring department in the past (makes you wonder how they got hired in the first place, but these types are out there at every airline).

Other factors to consider when asking for recommendation letters include the following: How well does this person know you? Has this person ever flown with you, and can he or she give an honest assessment of your flying skills? The best LORs to get are from people within the company you are applying to (i.e., internal recommendations), who know you very well and have flown with you often. They should be able to speak to not only your flying skills, but also your work ethic and personality on duty and off duty. I would give an LOR that meets all the aforementioned criteria a score of ten on a scale of one to ten, ten being the best. That doesn't mean that you should turn down a recommendation letter from someone within the company you are applying to who doesn't know you all that well. An LOR with a quality score of three is better than no LOR at all (except at UPS; see below for more detail about UPS LORs).

Over the course of a military-pilot career, it's quite normal to make great friends at one assignment but lose touch with them when they (or you) PCS to the next assignment. Facebook and social media have helped prevent this phenomenon to some degree, but it's still likely you will lose track of some friends along the way. A good way to find people you know within each airline is to use LinkedIn. If you don't already have an account, I highly recommend it (www.linkedin.com). I found a ton of pilots at various airlines whom I had lost touch with over the years by using the LinkedIn search feature. Simply type the name of the airline in the search bar at the top, and it will show all your LinkedIn contacts (and their contacts up to third order) who have the name of the airline you searched in their profile.

Another way to find old friends who are now airline pilots is to ask a pilot at that airline to send you the seniority lists for the different airframes and domiciles at that airline. You may recognize some names when you scan the seniority lists.

Don't feel bad about reaching out to an old friend or coworker you have not spoken to in years to hit him or her up for a recommendation letter. We've all been there, and we understand how the game is played. I have no problem writing a recommendation letter for long-lost acquaintances as long as it's somebody I would actually want to spend a four-day trip with at my airline. Ultimately, that's what it's all about. The airline industry is unique in that respect. We meet a coworker for the first time about thirty minutes before pushback on the first leg of a trip, and then we spend the next three to four days flying together and socializing after work. Therefore, the airline HR departments put forth a great deal of effort to make sure they are hiring people who play well with others and are easy to get along with. Nobody wants to spend four days working with a jerk, right?

Each airline seems to have different methods for submitting recommendation letters, and some have multiple methods, but they don't specify which method the applicant should use. For instance, many airline applications allow you to scan and upload your LORs as PDF attachments but also have a link that the person writing you an LOR can use to fill out a recommendation form online. In addition to the methods listed above, Southwest Airlines also has a way for their pilots to use the company internal communications server, called SWAlife, to fill out an internal recommendation form. Incidentally, Southwest Airlines won't read your LORs until after they interview you. Your best bet is to use all methods available. If an airline had several methods available for submitting recommendation letters, I tried to submit a couple LORs using each method.

UPS places more emphasis on the quality of a recommendation versus the quantity or number of LORs. They use a very lengthy internal employee-recommendation website form that can take over an hour to complete. Don't even think about asking someone to do this for you unless he or she knows you well and can speak to your flying skills.

I need to correct some now out-of-date information from *Cockpit to* Cockpit first edition regarding LORs. In the first edition, I stated that United Airlines wanted more LORs than most other airlines. They have since revised their policy. At the 2017 Women in Aviation International conference in Orlando, FL, a representative from United Airlines' HR team stated that four quality LORs (internal or external...makes no difference) from people who know you well and can speak to your flying skills will maximize the points available for LORs on the United Airlines pilot application.

No matter what method you use to submit LORs electronically, it's a good idea to also get original hard-copy ink-signature LORs (or at least a printout of letters that were signed, scanned, and e-mailed to you). You should carry these LORs to the interview if possible. JetBlue actually requires you to bring five hard-copy LORs to the interview. For my JetBlue interview, I printed all my LORs on very nice, heavyweight, light-blue résumé paper (they love all things Blue) and created a very professional LOR packet that included a table of contents. I have created an LOR table- of-contents template you can download from www.cockpit2cockpit.com as part of the *Cockpit to Cockpit* support package products.

There is certain etiquette to requesting letters of recommendation that, if applied correctly, will greatly improve your chances of actually receiving a letter of recommendation from each person you burden with the request. I purposely used the word "burden" because, let's face it, that's what it is. It takes time to write a quality recommendation letter. Everyone is busy with the thousands of other pieces of daily minutia in their lives, and you just added one more.

I highly recommend providing a draft LOR and résumé to each person from whom you are requesting a recommendation. It doesn't matter if they will be providing an electronic recommendation online or a normal paper recommendation letter. You are much more likely to receive an LOR if you provide them the 80 percent solution in the form of a draft letter versus making them do all the heavy lifting themselves. If they genuinely care, hopefully they will spend some time editing your words to make it more authentic and written in their own style, but at least you gave them a place to start. I have provided sample LORs in the support package products available on www.cockpit2cockpit.com to give you an idea of what an LOR should look like and what type of content should be included.

Let me be clear here, I am not advocating that you use the sample LORs provided in the Cockpit to Cockpit Support Package as your own by just changing certain items to match your information. That would be unethical and an ethical faux pas can easily lose you a great job. You need to draft your own unique LORs. I just provide examples to give you a place to start since you've never done this before and I want to save you some time and effort.

Here are a couple other ideas to increase the chance that someone will actually write you an LOR. If you're requesting an electronic recommendation, send them the link to the website. This works well with the pilotcredentials.com electronic recommendations by copying the "Recommendations" link from the top of the application homepage.

If the person is someone you worked with in the military, you should also provide the person copies of any performance reports from the time that you worked together. This will give him or her quick insight into your accomplishments, flying achievements, and contributions to the unit that he or she can speak to in their LOR.

When I was an air force officer, anytime I ever asked someone for a deliverable, I always asked for a reasonable suspense (also known as a "due date"). I find ten days is about right. Less than a week of turnaround time is too pushy; remember they are doing you a favor. Anything over two weeks and they will likely push it to the back burner and forget about it.

I recommend creating about ten different draft LOR templates that you can modify as needed. Unless you are a fighter pilot, most people find it very difficult to write about your own awesomeness, and even more difficult to write the same stuff ten different ways. Obviously you don't want the same version being used more than once with the same airline. It could be highly embarrassing and cost you a job interview if the hiring department at XYZ airline catches the fact that you have identical letters from more than one person. To avoid this mistake, I recommend keeping an LOR tracker to track which versions were used for each airline application. You can also use this same tracker to track whom you have sent LOR requests to and which have been received back. Trust me; it's easy to lose track of these details when you are applying to multiple airlines and you make multiple requests for LORs for each application. Sounds like a lot of work, right? Well, guess what? I have included an LOR tracker template in the support package products available on www.cockpit2cockpit.com.

Résumé? What's That?

For many of you, this may be the first time in your life you need to create a résumé or even interview for a job! I know that was the case for me, and I found the process a little (OK, a lot) intimidating. Don't let it scare you. I'm going to let you in on a little secret...the airlines don't care too much about the format of your résumé. They just need a way to get some basic overview information about your background, education, and flying career.

There is no need to pay a résumé service or download a résumé template from an internet service. In fact, that may not even work, since airline-pilot résumés tend to be a little different from the standard business-world résumé. All you really need is to get your hands on a few example résumés from friends or coworkers who got hired by an airline, pick and choose the best ideas from each, and then create your own in a similar style. Once you have a draft, your interview preparation company (see chapter 8 for more information about interview-preparation services), if you choose to use one, will be happy to review it and provide you feedback. You may also choose to use a professional résumé and application review service such as Checked and Set (www.checkedandset.net...see chapter 7 for additional information).

There is no "one size fits all" format when it comes to airline-pilot résumés. Any professional-looking format should suffice. However, there are a few dos and don'ts and helpful hints involved. Once again, because this book is all about saving you time and effort, I have included a sample résumé template in the *Cockpit to Cockpit* support package for you to use as a starting point. All support package products are available for purchase on our website www.cockpit2cockpit.com.

The number-one rule of airline résumés is don't go over *one* page. I know what you're about to say..."How is that possible when I'm so awesome and I've done so many great things that the airline just has to know about?" Trust me; they don't need to know about every officer performance report (OPR) bullet in your ROP, and they don't care. Your résumé is going to be looked at for less than 30 seconds; they don't have time to read all that fluff. Keep it to one page and make it look clean and organized. Help them find the key information they care about by using bold font and organizing your résumé in a way that makes the important information jump out at them. As we walk through the various sections of a great airline résumé, you can refer to the example in figure 3.

Joseph C. Pilot

1234 Badass Street
Idaho Falls, ID 67890

(555) 555-5555 cell
joseph.pilot@gmail.com

SUMMARY	***Professional pilot with over 25 years of civilian and military fighter/trainer flying experience. Proven military leader, instructor and evaluator pilot with unique communication and diplomacy experience.***

QUALIFICATIONS

Airline Transport Pilot	Air Force Safety Trained	FAA First Class Medical
B-737 Type Rating	F-16, T-6, T-37 IP	Valid US Passport
CFII (AMEL)	F-16 SEFE	FCC Restricted Permit

Total Time: 4890	Instructor:	2101	PIC:	3968	Instrument:	301
(.3 conversion factor)	Turbine PIC:	3745	MEL:	1565	Combat:	296

WORK HISTORY

Aug 2014 – Present	**BE-55, AA-5 Flight Instructor (AMEL)**, Aviation Flight Academy, Idaho Falls, ID
Aug 2010 – Aug 2014	**T-6 Instructor Pilot**, 80th Flying Training Wing (FTW), Sheppard AFB, TX Pilot Instructor Trainer, Euro-NATO Joint Jet Pilot Training United States Senior National Representative, 80 FTW Chief of Commander's Action Group
Jan 2008 – Aug 2010	**F-16 Flight Examiner**, 12th Air Force (AF), Davis-Monthan AFB, AZ 12 AF Standardization/Evaluation (Stan/Eval) Fighter Branch Chief, 12th AF Mission Briefer, Volunteer combat deployment Operation IRAQI FREEDOM
Feb 2005 – Jan 2008	**F-16 Instructor Pilot**, 77th Fighter Squadron, Shaw AFB, SC Assistant Director of Operations, Deputy Chief of Wing Plans/Inspections, Operation NOBLE EAGLE Alert Pilot, F-16 East Coast Demonstration Team Safety Officer
Aug 2001 – Feb 2005	**T-37 Instructor Pilot**, 80th Flying Training Squadron, Sheppard AFB, TX Flight Commander, Military Training Officer, Supervisor of Flying, Air Show Coordinator
Jul 2000 – Aug 2001	**F-16 4-Ship Flight Lead**, 80th Fighter Squadron, Kunsan AB, Republic of Korea Chief of Scheduling, Sensitive Reconnaissance Operations Alert Force Pilot
Nov 1997 – Jul 2000	**F-16 2-Ship Flight Lead**, 77th Fighter Squadron, Shaw AFB, SC Chief of Training, Volunteer combat deployment Operations NORTHERN WATCH / SOUTHERN WATCH
EDUCATION	Air War College, Distance Learning, 2011 Air Command and Staff College, Distance Learning, 2008 MS, Aeronautical Science, Embry-Riddle Aeronautical University, 2004, GPA 4.0 BS, Aeronautical Science, Embry-Riddle Aeronautical University, 1995, GPA 3.57
ACHIEVEMENTS	77th Fighter Squadron *Top Gun Award*, low angle bombing event, 2007 *Cragg Award*, best overall 4-Ship Flight Lead, air-to-air competition, 2001 77th Fighter Squadron *Wingman of the Quarter*, 1999 29/29 Air Force check rides graded Q1 (highest qualification), 5 commendables Air Medal (2), three flawless combat weapons deliveries
VOLUNTEER WORK, HOBBIES, COMMUNITY SERVICE	Order of Daedalians Texoma Flight 29 Scholarship Officer, Civil Air Patrol Senior Member, Scuba Diving, Camping, Hiking, Travel, Cycling, Reading, Fitness Habitat for Humanity, Christmas in Action, Girls in Flight (GIFT) Academy

Figure 3. Sample résumé

The key information they will look for are your certificates and qualifications (ATP, CFII, FAA Class I Medical, any type ratings, etc.), a breakdown of your flight time, a brief scan of your assignments and work history to look for aircraft flown and the highest qualification achieved in each aircraft (aircraft commander, IP, evaluator, etc.), highest degree earned and GPA, and anything else that helps you stand out from other applicants (volunteer work, achievements, etc.).

Here are a few helpful hints as you sit down to start creating what is likely your first résumé for a job in the civilian world. Make sure you put your name and contact information at the top of the page. Seems pretty commonsense, right? Confession time...on my first draft, I started working on the main body of my résumé first, figuring that I would go back and pretty it up later with all the formalities. I was so proud when I finally reached a draft that fit on one page and included all my wonderful achievements, until I realized that I forgot to leave room for my contact information at the top of the page...*doh!* There's a sure way to make sure your résumé ends up in the "Do Not Hire" Pile. Fortunately, I caught it before I uploaded and attached it to my applications. Your contact information should include your name, address, telephone number, and e-mail. Make sure the contact information on your résumé matches the contact information you provided on your application.

Throughout your résumé you should emphasize your leadership experience. Leadership experience has become a high interest item with airline recruiters lately. You can do this by listing leadership positions held in the "Employment History" section, leadership awards in the "Awards/Achievements" section, and any leadership positions associated with volunteer activities in the "Community Service/Volunteer Work" section.

Here's another time-saving tip for you. When I first started the application process, I had an objective statement at the top of my résumé that said something to the effect of:

OBJECTIVE: To obtain career employment as a pilot with XYZ airline

There are several problems with using an objective statement on your résumé. The first is that it then requires you to create a separate résumé for every airline you apply to, which can lead to a major faux pas if you upload the wrong version to a different airline application and forget to change XYZ to ABC.

The second problem is, it's redundant *and unnecessary*. Obviously you want to be a pilot for XYZ airline; otherwise, why would you be submitting an application? I can just hear the hiring manager saying out loud as he or she reads the objective statement: "Really, Captain Obvious? No shit you want to be a pilot here!" as they place my résumé in the trash.

The third problem is it's an outdated résumé technique. Most résumé experts (disclaimer: I'm not a résumé expert, but I did stay at a Holiday Inn Express last night) would probably recommend you use a summary statement instead. A summary statement gives the reader a quick, two-or-three-sentence summary of your overall aviation experience and qualifications. Here is a good example of a summary statement:

> *Professional pilot with over 25 years of military and civilian flying background in fighters and trainers. Proven military leader, instructor and evaluator pilot with unique communication and diplomacy experience.*

The summary statement allows you to use the same résumé for every airline you apply to. Just make sure the body of your résumé supports anything you are trying to highlight in your summary.

Somewhere near the top of your résumé, you will want to include sections titled "Flight Time" and "Certificates/Ratings." The titles aren't so important; you can use different verbiage, but make sure this info is included on your résumé near the top, because this info is hugely important to the hiring department.

You will want to provide your total flight time and a breakdown of your more important times. A few that you should definitely include are multiengine time, turbine time, PIC time, turbine PIC, and combat time (a great differentiator for military pilots). I highly recommend you use a .3 conversion factor (per sortie) on your résumé flight times also. Remember, you are competing with civilian pilots for these jobs. Civilian pilots have the advantage of logging their engine-running time on the ground in their flight times. Yep, unlike us military pilots, civilians get flight-time credit for sitting on the ground burning fuel. As you know, our military flight time only includes time in the air plus a five-minute taxi time for each sortie (in most aircraft). Therefore, give yourself every advantage you can by adding the .3 conversion factor to each sortie (not to each flight hour...that's a common mistake the airlines look for). Don't worry; nobody at the airline is going to accuse you of "speeding" for using a conversion factor on your résumé flight times. In fact, they may accuse you of being a moron, if you don't use a conversion factor!

If your flight times include a combination of military and civilian flight time, you might want to create a spreadsheet to justify how you derived your flight times listed on your résumé (this is more for the interview). I have included a Résumé Hours Conversion Spreadsheet in the support package products available on our website www.cockpit2cockpit.com.

The "Certificates/Ratings" section (some people label this section as "Qualifications") includes all your FAA and FCC ratings such as your ATP, CFII, type ratings, FAA First Class Medical, and FCC Restricted Radiotelephone Permit. If you have an ATP, there is no need to list commercial or instrument ratings, since the ATP supersedes these. A good technique is to look up the airline's minimum requirements for pilots (usually listed on the application website) and include them in this section.

The largest section of your résumé should be your work history and/or experience. This is where you will list your job history in reverse chronological order starting with your most recent or current job. For military pilots, a good technique is to break out each permanent change of station (PCS) assignment going back to your first operational flying assignment. There is no need to list initial pipeline training (flying training assignments prior to your first operational assignment such as Undergraduate Pilot Training, Introduction to Fighter Fundamentals, etc.). You old farts who have too many PCS assignments to fit on one page may need to get more creative and combine several assignments into one, grouped by aircraft type flown.

Here you will create two columns. The far-left column will have the month/year date range for each assignment. The next column will summarize your accomplishments at each assignment starting with the aircraft type flown and the highest qualification achieved in that assignment listed in bold font (remember, you want the most important info to jump off the page at the reader). After that, you should very briefly summarize the various leadership positions and additional duties held during that assignment. Keep it brief; the reader is more than likely only going to look for the info you already highlighted in bold font. The rest is just fluff. If you choose to skip the awards and/or achievements section of your résumé, you may consider sprinkling the more important ones into this section.

Also, try to avoid any unexplained missing time periods in your chronological sequence of work history. That can raise questions with potential employers.

An education section is also a must. Although most airlines don't have an advanced-degree requirement, it is a great differentiator that will help you get hired...and not just for an airline job. I highly recommend getting your master's degree knocked out before you leave the military. In addition to listing your school, dates, and type of degree earned, you will also want to include your GPA (unless it's really bad) and any academic honors (magna cum laude, piña colada, etc.).

As you get toward the bottom of your **one page and only one page résumé** (see how the bold font really grabs the reader's attention?), you can get a little creative with other optional résumé sections.

"Achievements/Awards" is a very common section that you could use. Although you may have some awards that greatly helped your military career (e.g., Field Grade Officer of the Year), the fact is they don't mean much to the airline industry. Remember, they are hiring you to be a pilot. Try to stick to flying-related awards. See figure 3 for some good examples.

A good technique is to also include a "Volunteer Service" or "Community Service" section. If you can show that you enjoy doing things that are not just about yourself, things that give back to the community, or that you are passionate about a good cause or volunteering with your church, mosque, synagogue, and so on, it indicates to the airlines that you are a person of high moral character. This will definitely help you stand out from other applicants. Two airlines in particular that I know are huge on this are Southwest and JetBlue, and I suspect most of the other major airlines like to see it also.

On the other hand, if you are a cold-hearted, uncaring bastard, then a good technique is to list a "Hobbies/Interests" section instead. I'm kidding, of course, but the reality is that some of us type-A military pilots tend to invest our whole selves into our career and striving to become the best military aviator possible. Add in the time suck of raising a family (oh my, did I just call family a time suck?), getting an advanced degree, and completing PME, and there just isn't much time left for volunteer service. Listing hobbies and interests on your résumé essentially serves the same purpose as a "Volunteer Service" section. It helps differentiate you from other applicants and provides some icebreaker material you can use in the interview. Then you can use that icebreaker to tell them what a great human being you are. For example:

Interviewer: So, John, I see here on your résumé that you are an avid surfer; tell me about that.

You: Oh yes, I love to surf. Just last week I was catching a gnarly wave when I spotted a young boy who seemed to be drowning. Well, I steered my longboard over to him, and that's when I saw the shark fin heading straight for him. Without even thinking, I leapt into the water and fought off a six-foot mako shark with my bare hands until he swam away. Then I put the little boy on my board and towed him in to shore by swimming against the riptide. When I got him to the beach, I realized he was unconscious, so I performed CPR and brought him back to life. It was totally radical! His parents offered me a $100,000 reward, but I was like, "Naw, I'm just happy I got to him before that shark."

Interviewer: You're hired!

I see a lot of people put an "Availability Date" section on their résumé also. That's OK if you need to fill the space, but if you're struggling to fit everything you want into just one page, you can skip the availability date. It's on your application and therefore redundant *and unnecessary*.

As you can see, writing a résumé isn't as hard or intimidating as it first appeared. You will go through a few drafts as you fine-tune your masterpiece. Make sure you have your spouse, a friend, or a professional airline application/résumé review service look it over with a critical eye before you upload it and attach it to your application.

List of References

Your reference list is probably not an actual piece of paperwork that the airline will ask for. However, most airlines will ask for references on your application, so it is handy to gather your reference contact information ahead of time. You will need to provide the name, address, phone number, and e-mail address for each of your listed references. In addition, if your reference is an airline pilot, you may also be required to provide his or her employee number.

How many references is enough? I recommend gathering contact info for five personal and five professional references. If you can find a few references that work at each airline you are applying to, that's a bonus, but not totally necessary. It's also a good idea to let people know you have listed them as a reference so they aren't caught off guard when the airlines call them. Also let them know that under no circumstances are they to discuss that college-fraternity or sorority trip to Panama City!

Creating a list of references is not rocket surgery, but I wrote this book because I want to simplify the military-to-airline transition for you. Therefore, I have created a List of References template that you can download as part of the support package products available on our website www.cockpit2cockpit.com.

Summary

Well, that's it; now that you have gathered all the required paperwork, you're ready to sit down and start filling out applications. I know what you're thinking..."Finally!" You thought I would never get to the important part. If you were the type of kid who peeked at his or her Christmas presents, you may have been tempted to skip chapters 1 through 5. But for those of you good boys and girls who patiently followed directions and read this book from the beginning, you now realize that your chances of success go up exponentially if you're willing to do the preparation work. After all, you wouldn't jump right into the Before-Takeoff Checklist without running the Exterior Preflight, Interior Preflight, Before Engine Start, and Before Taxi checklists, would you?...Would you?

THE CHECKLIST

- **Obtain three to five official copies of all high-school and college transcripts.**
- **Obtain your actual flight-evaluation folder or copies of the contents (documentation of your performance on all your military flight evaluations).**
- **Obtain your actual military flight records or copies of the contents (documentation of all your military flight time including individual sorties).**
- **Prepare your logbooks for the interview. If you have an electronic logbook, print a copy in the format you will use for the interview so you understand how to do it when the time comes.**
- **Make sure your passport is current or obtain a passport if you don't have one.**
- **Obtain a copy of your National Driver's Registry report and driving records from any state in which you have been issued a driver's license.**
- **Apply for an FCC Radiotelephone Operator's Permit.**

- **Obtain an FAA First Class Medical.**
- **Request a copy of your FAA airman's medical and flying records.**
- **Request and gather three to five recommendation letters for each airline you are applying to.**
- **Create a letter of recommendation tracker spreadsheet.**
- **Develop a one-page airline-application résumé using the advice and techniques contained in this chapter.**
- **Create a list of personal and professional references.**

CHAPTER 6

Applications

YOU'RE PROBABLY THINKING, "Wow, more than half way through this book and I haven't even submitted an application yet." I appreciate your patience in hanging with me up to this point. I promise, we're really close. But before we sit down to the computer and start working on our applications, there is one more housekeeping chore we need to accomplish first.

Submitting an airline application is a lot like saying "F$@!" in front of your mom. Once it's out there, you can't take it back. The minute you hit send on an airline application, you are vulnerable to public scrutiny by the airline HR department. They now have your name, email address, employment history, and much more. They know what schools you attended, where you have lived, what military units you have served in...basically everything about you. So before we start working on our airline applications, the first thing we need to do is to clean up our online image.

Sanitize Your Social Media Profile

It is really important to clean up your social media profiles before you hit send on your first airline application. Any material that might be considered offensive or off-color needs to be removed (that covers about 98% of most pilot's social media posts). Also remove all those party pictures with drink in hand. I was amazed when I went to clean up my Facebook page just how many pictures had alcohol in them. I know you don't have a drinking problem, and you know you don't have a drinking problem, but the human resources folks at XYZ airline may not know that you don't have a drinking problem.

Google yourself, to make sure you get a chance to see everything that's out there about you before your potential employer does it. It might not be enough to just clean up your own social media profile. You may have some prankster friends who have posted some not so flattering pictures of you after a few too many. Maybe you have a crazy ex-whatever who decided to take some revenge on you by slandering your good name or image online? You may not even know it's out there. If that statement doesn't make you think twice about ever sending your boyfriend or girlfriend a naked picture text message, I don't know what will. If you're extremely concerned about your past coming back to haunt you, consider hiring a professional service to help you clean up your online image.

When to Apply

One of the most common questions with respect to applications is how long prior to separating or retiring from the military you should submit your applications. The answer is…wait for it…it depends. It depends on your availability date. Your availability date will be discussed in more detail later in this chapter, but it is essentially the date you tell the airline you are available to start training. You may recall from chapter 4 that you can actually start airline training while on military terminal leave. As a general rule of thumb, about one year prior to your availability date is ideal to submit your applications.

If your application is competitive (and it should be if you have been following the advice in this book), you should start getting some interview invitations within about six months of your availability date. In general, the closer you get to your availability date, the greater your chances of getting an interview call.

Application Windows

One of the things that came as a surprise to me as I began my airline application process was the fact that some airlines have "application windows" that open and close with little or no notice. In English that translates to…even though you are ready to apply to your dream airline, they may not be accepting applications at this time. Getting information about when various airline application windows will open and close can be frustrating because they usually don't advertise it, and if they do it's often on short notice. I have seen airline application windows open for as short as forty-eight hours, so when you find out that a window is open, don't delay getting your application submitted.

In general, the legacy (Delta, American, and United) windows are on a continuously open status and should remain that way, barring any industry shakeups, due to the high number of projected mandatory retirements in the near future. However, one thing remains certain in this industry: nothing is certain!

One of the best ways I found to stay up-to-date on airline application windows was to become a member of Future & Active Pilot Advisors (FAPA). As a member, you can take advantage of e-mail and text notifications when application windows open. FAPA has several tiers of membership starting at $49 and includes services such as résumé review, job-fair notification and discounts, interview preparation, and access to a database of current information on each airline. You can check it out for yourself at www.fapa.aero.

If you don't want to shell out the $49, there are a few other ways to stay "in the know." One of those is the good old-fashioned "bro" network (and I mean than in the most gender-neutral sense of the phrase). If you have friends who work at the airline you are interested in, they will usually know when an application window is about to open or close.

When you join TPN, your "bro" network grows to over 15,000 pilots (at last count and still growing). If an airline you are interested in does not have a window currently opened, you can ask on TPN if anyone knows when XYZ airlines will open their next window and you should get a pretty quick response.

Where to Apply

As we discussed earlier in this book, there are a couple third-party airline application websites that you will likely use if you are targeting any of the major airlines. Delta, United, and many of the regional airlines (Air Wisconsin, Compass, Endeavor, Envoy, Express Jet, Mesa, and Republic Airways to name a few) use www.airlineapps.com. The cost of Airline Apps is approximately $60 per year. One of the things I liked about this website is that data-entry windows are not character limited, thus allowing you to use a generous character count to enter job descriptions, achievements, and so on.

The other commonly used third-party airline application website is www.pilotcredentials.com. Pilot Credentials is used for applications with FedEx, Southwest, American Airlines, and PSA. It costs approximately $60 per year. Unlike Airline Apps, the airlines that use Pilot Credentials each maintain separate websites located at www.fedex.pilotcredentials.com, www.swa.pilotcredentials.com, and www.aa.pilotcredentials.com. The $60 annual fee provides access to all three-airline application websites. There is a way to enter general application data into the Global Pilot Credentials site and have it imported to the Southwest Airlines, FedEx, and American Airlines sites; however, I've heard from several pilots who had some problems doing it that way. I just went to each of the three sites individually and filled out applications. As opposed to the Airline Apps website, Pilot Credentials data-entry windows are very character limited. You will need to be concise with job descriptions, achievements, and so on.

There are a couple of things to be aware of with the Southwest Application in particular. In addition to applying on www.swa.pilotcredentials.com, Southwest requires that you also create a profile on the Southwest.com website using the "Careers" link at the bottom of the page. This will take you into the Southwest ICIMS system where you can create a pilot candidate profile. You will need to do this when Southwest has an application window opened. Search for the keyword "pilot" and apply to the specific requisition number for the pilot job position that is advertised. If Southwest subsequently closes the application window, you will have to repeat this process again during the next open window by applying to the new pilot job requisition number.

As previously mentioned, Pilot Credentials data-entry windows are very character limited. However, when you get to the questionnaire located at the end of the Southwest application, there is a question that asks, "Any additional information about your flying or work experience that you want to provide?" I discovered that this one data-entry field was not as character limited as the others. This is a good place to discuss volunteer, charity work, and achievements.

If the airline you are targeting does not use one of the third-party application websites listed above, then you should be able to apply directly through the airline's main public website (the one they use to book tickets). Try searching "careers" or "jobs" or "work here" from within the airline website. There is usually a link in small font located at the bottom of the main page.

In addition to the websites mentioned above for submitting your applications, Delta and American also use specific sites for communicating information to pilot candidates. Delta has a Facebook group called Delta Air Lines Pilot Recruiting. They use their Facebook group to send out pilot recruiting event announcements and registration. American Airlines has a separate recruiting website used for similar purposes. They call it the American Airlines Talent Runway and it can be found at www.talent.aa.com.

Miscellaneous Application Queep

One of the first things you will do on your application is create a profile with all your basic contact information including your e-mail address. If you don't have a professional e-mail address that uses your name (e.g., first.last@gmail.com), I highly encourage you to establish one to use exclusively for your airline applications. Not that there's anything wrong with fighterguy69@yahoo.com—it probably works great on Tinder for that casual hookup—but it won't get you an airline job.

The other problem with a complicated e-mail address is that there is a human on the other end who is eventually going to review your application, and humans are prone to error. My friend Rob almost lost out on his dream job with American Airlines because somebody in HR copied down his phone number wrong; they were off by one digit. Back in Rob's day the chief pilot used to personally call pilot candidates for interview invites. The only way Rob found out that American Airlines was trying to call him was by finding a ten-day-old missed-call note in his squadron inbox. Lucky for Rob, American Airlines called his work phone number, and eventually they were able to reach him. If that can happen with a phone number, it can certainly happen with a complicated e-mail address. You may not be as lucky as Rob, so use the first.last@e-mailprovider.com format to minimize the risk of an error.

While I'm on the subject of e-mail, make sure you set up your e-mail spam filters to accept e-mails from each of the airlines you apply to. One of the ways you will know that an airline is interested in you is they will e-mail you asking for more information or ask you to correct an error on your application. Wouldn't it suck if your e-mail program sent that e-mail to your spam folder because it looked like marketing junk that airlines send out all the time?

This has been a problem with the American Airlines application in particular. American Airlines has a unique step in their interview process known as a video interview. American sends out a video-interview link via e-mail to prospective candidates. If they like your video interview, then you get invited to travel to Dallas for a face-to-face interview. I have several friends who reported that their video interview invite e-mail went to their spam folder. In addition to setting your e-mail filters to accept e-mails from your targeted airlines, it's not a bad idea to also check your spam folder daily in case it gets past your filters for some reason.

As you dig in to applications, you will find they can take quite a bit of time. One thing that may save you some time is to get a copy of your most recent security-clearance application from the military. This will come in handy on the application when it asks for supervisor names, contact info, work and residential address history, and so on.

In order to help cut down the amount of time you spend filling out each application, you might want to make a Microsoft Word document that contains much of the basic info that will be required on each application. That way you can just cut and paste the information from the Word document to another application. Information such as your residential address history, job descriptions, work address history, and supervisor names and telephone numbers are things that will be required on most applications.

Once you have triple-checked your application and you are 100 percent sure it is ready to hit the "submit" button, make sure you print a copy for yourself before submitting electronically. You will often find errors in print that you didn't see electronically. It is likely that the airline HR department will print the applications they want to screen in more detail for potential interviews, so they will be looking at the same thing you will see when you print from the application website (most airline application websites include instructions for printing your application). This is how I discovered that most data-entry windows on Pilot Credentials were character limited... that is, most of my data got cut off. I then had to go back and shorten my responses until they fit in the provided space when printed.

Another consideration before hitting the "submit" button is to determine if what you are about to do is irreversible. By that I mean that some applications, once submitted, are then locked, and you won't be able to go back and make changes later. That's not the case with most airline applications. Both Pilot Credentials and Airlines Apps do allow you to make changes, update flying hours, and so on after submitting your application. Some of the airline applications that don't allow changes after submitting include UPS, Spirit, Atlas, and Alaska Airlines. Airlines change their applications and hiring process all the time, so don't take my word for it on which airline applications are able to be updated later and which are not. If you are unsure, call the HR department and ask before you hit the "submit" button.

Airline-Specific Application Reindeer Games

While most airline applications are pretty straightforward, a few have some unique sections that are worth discussing here. The American Airlines application (aa.pilotcredentials.com) includes a section called Organizational

Fit Assessment (OFA). It is essentially a personality screening to determine if you will be a good fit with the culture of American Airlines. It consists of two sections. The first section includes several hundred true/false questions such as:

I like cats	T or F?
I hate most people	T or F?
I don't like working with clowns	T or F?

The second section consists of scenario-based multiple-choice questions such as:

> You are on the second day of a three-day trip, and you have noticed that your captain does not wear his required uniform hat. What do you do?
>
> A. I won't wear my hat for the rest of the trip. I do everything I see my captain do.
> B. I ask my captain if he has a religious objection to wearing headgear, because I am very sensitive to other cultures and beliefs.
> C. I call the chief pilot and tell him my captain is a flagrant rule breaker.
> D. Just after gear-up on departure, I will turn to him and say, "So, boss, what's up with not following the uniform standards?"

I wish I could give you some advice on how to prepare for the OFA, but since I never got a call from American, I don't think I'm qualified to tell you what they are looking for. My gut instinct (and the advice everyone gave me) is to answer honestly, not the way you think they want you to answer. Don't overthink it. As long as there is nothing wrong with you, you should be fine.

As I discussed earlier, if American Airlines likes your application and wants to consider you for an interview, they will e-mail you a link and instructions for a video interview (this is the e-mail that sometimes gets sent to the spam folder). The instructions will tell you that you must complete the video interview within five days. If you pass the video interview, then you will get invited for a real face-to-face interview. There is no human interaction; your responses get recorded, and the American Airlines pilot-hiring team will review them at a later time. You will be read each question by a prerecorded voice and given thirty seconds to think about your response; then the recording starts. You have three minutes to answer each question. The video interview is pretty simple, and most everybody passes it, but here are a couple simple rules to follow.

Dress as though this is the real interview. A conservative suit and tie (for men) is appropriate. Now is not the time to show off your individuality by wearing surfer shorts and playing Jimmy Buffet music in the background. Make sure you are in a professional-looking, distraction-free environment with excellent Wi-Fi capability. The good folks at American probably won't be too impressed if they hear the TV blaring or the dog barking in the background.

If you know someone who has interviewed recently at American, you might want to ask what questions he or she got asked before attempting the video interview yourself. You can also probably find some gouge on the Internet by searching "American Airlines video interview." Incidentally, JetBlue has recently added a video interview as part of their hiring process also.

Computer-Application Scoring

It's no secret that the largest US airlines (and several smaller air carriers) use computer algorithms to screen and score pilot applications and résumés. When Delta, American, United, and Southwest opened their hiring windows in the fall of 2013 and early 2014, they were flooded with over ten thousand pilot applications each (mind you, it was probably the same ten thousand pilots applying to each airline). Similar stories followed suit at other large air carriers who have opened hiring windows since then. In an effort to sift through these thousands of applications, these airlines have adopted computer software to apply a numeric score to each application and/or résumé based on tailored criteria specific to each airline, such as flying hours, flying positions held (instructor, evaluator, flight lead, aircraft commander, etc.), leadership positions held, FAA certificates and ratings, highest education level achieved,

GPA, number of recommendation letters, availability date, and numerous other factors.

When the airline is ready to interview applicants, they will set a cutoff application score and look only at those applications above the cutoff to evaluate for potential interview invites. The following are just hypothetical numbers to help you understand how this process works. For example, if the maximum application score is 400, an airline might use a score of 300 as the cutoff. They will have the computer software show them only the applications that scored above 300. Let's just say that yields 1000 applications, but they only plan to hire 500 pilots for the year, and historically 30 percent of those interviewed will not pass the interview. Therefore, the airline will invite 715 candidates to interview throughout the year to fill 500 training slots. They will then manually review the 1000 applications and résumés that scored above 300 and determine which lucky 715 applicants will get an interview invite (actually a few more than that since some of those invited to interview will decline, usually because they already got hired somewhere else).

So now I'm going to give you some techniques that will help improve your application score. They won't guarantee you a job, but they will increase your chances of getting an interview. The rest is up to you. Do these techniques really work? Well, all I can tell you is that when I first submitted my applications, I was not armed with these techniques, and I wasn't getting any calls. Within two weeks of applying these techniques (that a friend passed along to me), the phone started ringing. Disclaimer: you still need to have the raw credentials (flying hours, positions held, FAA certificates/ratings, education, etc.) to really make it work.

The first thing you should do is to check as many boxes as possible (except the "Any DUIs?" box…that probably won't win you any points). Some may not seem like they apply to you, but they do. For instance, the certificates-and-ratings section the application may ask if you have an English Proficiency associated with your ATP. Of course you do; it says so right on the back of your license. There may be a question on the application that asks if you have ever been a check airman. If you have been an evaluator in your aircraft, then answer *yes!* Obviously you don't want to lie about anything, but if you can easily defend why you checked a box on your application during the interview, then by all means check that box! It's better to be sitting in the interview explaining why you checked the box than to not be at the interview at all, right?

There are also a lot of boxes you can check by getting certain civilian flight ratings via the FAA Military Competency test. Even if you never plan to do any civilian flight instructing, if you have ever been an instructor in a military aircraft, then you might as well get your CFII certificate just by taking the FAA Military Competency Test (see chapter 2 for additional information about the MCT).

Another easy square to fill on an airline application is the tail-wheel endorsement. You can go to just about any local airport and get a tail-wheel endorsement added to your logbook with as few as three to five hours of flight instruction. Remember, every square you fill adds points to your application.

I'm sure you are saying to yourself, "OK, fill as many squares as possible…got it. But I only have so many I can fill…then what?" Well, here are the real magic beans…they are called *keywords*. This is where you can really make your money on beating the computer…uh, I mean improving your application score. The computer actually adds points to your application every time it sees certain keywords. So what are these magic keywords? The answer is I don't know, but I know what things the airlines are looking for, and I'm willing to bet that words associated with an airline's core values are included in the list of keywords. Here is a list of some keywords that will likely add points to your application:

Team
Leader
IP/Instructor Pilot
Crew Resource Management
EP/Evaluator Pilot
Volunteer
FE/Flight Examiner
Safety
#1/#XXX
Honor(able)
Flight Lead
AC/Aircraft Commander
Combat
Supervisor
Commander
Distinguished Graduate
Mission Commander
Deployed
Air Medal
Award

Courage	Conscientious
Selfless	Warrior
Productive	Integrity
Work Ethic	Loyal(ty)
Ethical	

Of course, this list is not all-inclusive; I'm sure you can think of many other words that an airline might look for to help them differentiate applications.

Here is a quick example of how you can sprinkle these keywords into your application. Somewhere in the application, it will ask you to list your employment history. Since most of us military pilots went right into military service after college, listing each military assignment as a separate employment is usually acceptable. Let's say for example that on one of those assignments, you served as the chief of scheduling in your C-130 squadron. "Chief of scheduling" gets you zero keyword points. So instead you might list your job title as "C-130 **Aircraft Commander**/Chief of Scheduling." One keyword point. Always lead your job title with the highest aircraft qualification held in that assignment. Remember, the airlines are hiring you to be a pilot, not a shoe clerk.

For each job, the application will also ask you to describe your key responsibilities in that job. You might be tempted to write, "Responsible for scheduling 23 pilots and 12 aircraft for over 20,000 flying hours annually." Although that sounds very impressive to you, to the computer it sounds like zero keyword points. Instead, consider using something like this: "**Leader** for a **team** of five flight schedulers." Do you see how you easily worked one keyword into the job title and two more into the job-responsibilities description?

As you can see, the more jobs you list, the more opportunity you have to input some keywords. Therefore, it is to your benefit to list as many jobs as possible. A creative way to lengthen your employment history section is to break out lengthy deployments that occurred within a military assignment as separate military assignments. You should also list your entire employment history going back to high school, including non-flying jobs. Delta in particular is big on this.

It will give you more opportunities to use keywords, list leadership positions, and demonstrate work ethic. Yes, it will take you more time and it's a pain in the ass to dig up information going that far back, but as you know by now... **getting a job is a full-time job**.

Another place to potentially score some points is the education-history section. I'm operating on the premise that the computer gives you some points for each entry. As a military officer, there are tons of formal training schools, TDY/TADs, and PMEs that you can list in the education-history section. I recommend including any formal flight-training course, including UPT. You can also include any safety courses, CRM courses, and so on. Also, don't forget about PME regardless of whether you took the course in residence or correspondence.

Common Application Errors

There are a few areas to watch out for on an airline application. Errors in these sections can mean the difference between getting an interview and not...so be careful and check your work.

"Address History" is a section that is often screwed up. The application will ask you to provide your residential address history for the past X years. One way to screw this up is to not provide them the requested time frame—for example, if they ask for 10 years of address history and you only go back 9.75 years.

Another way to screw it up is to have overlapping dates for subsequent addresses...that is, you tell them you lived at 123 Green Street from 3/15/11 to 6/25/14, and then you list your next address as 456 Blue Street from 6/1/14 to present. Notice that those two date ranges overlap, indicating that either you lived in two places at once or you're a moron unworthy of employment at this airline.

Yet another way to screw it up, and this is probably the most common error, is to leave a time gap between two addresses. Here is how this one often gets screwed up. Let's say you had two weeks of TDY/TAD training en route between assignments. You moved out of residence A on 3/1/15, but due to the two weeks of training en route, you didn't move in to residence B until 3/15/15. The computer will probably flag your application as having an error and therefore not provide it a score, thereby taking you out of consideration for an interview. You may or may not get an e-mail from the airline, asking you to correct this error. In that scenario, I would just list the dates sequentially with no time gap…that is, I would say I lived at residence A until 3/14/15, and I began residence B on 3/15/15. If it's a lengthy time gap in between (more than thirty days), then I would list a third address (even if it was just temporary) in between to keep the dates sequential.

The same principal of sequential dates with no time gaps can be applied to the "Employment History" section. So what do you do if you were truly unemployed for a period of time? Most applications will tell you to list your unemployment period as a separate entry and ask you to explain what you were doing during that unemployed time. This most often comes up for military pilots after they separate or retire and before they are hired by an airline. It's not a big deal to list a period of unemployment; just make sure your dates, including unemployment periods, are sequential with no gaps.

Some airlines will also ask for a copy of your military evaluations. Delta Airlines is one that definitely will ask for this. Don't worry if your résumé dates, OPR dates, and application dates (in terms of address and job history) don't all exactly match each other. Just make sure on the application that they are listed sequentially with no overlap or gaps.

The "Flight Times" section is another common place for errors. The best way to avoid errors here is to read the directions very carefully. You may recall that when we talked about the résumé in chapter 5, I told you to use a .3 conversion factor per military sortie. You may or may not be allowed to do that on your application. Some websites tell you to do so; others don't. AirlineApps.com (used by Delta, United, and other smaller airlines) specifically directs that you *must not* add a conversion factor. **Unless the website instructions specifically tell you to apply a conversion factor, don't do it!** You don't want to have to explain in the interview why your logbook totals don't match your application.

If you are allowed to apply a conversion factor, an electronic logbook will be very handy at this point. I added a custom column to my electronic logbook so that I could log sorties. It was pretty simple; I logged one sortie for each military flight (two if we air-refueled between training events). It was then very easy to use the filters in my electronic-logbook software to count the number of sorties I had for each subcategory of flight time on the application (total, night, PIC, MEL, IP, etc.).

Another common error is improperly logging PIC time that does not meet the airline's definition of PIC. In chapter 3 we discussed the fact that for hiring purposes, most airlines define PIC time differently from the FAA. Most airlines define PIC as time logged as captain/aircraft commander, or the person who retains overall authority for the safety of the aircraft. Make sure the times you enter meet the definition they are looking for.

If you have chosen to rely solely on military flight records for your interview instead of a logbook (which is perfectly acceptable; refer to pros and cons in chapter 3), then you will have some flight times required on the application that are not included in your military flight records. Some examples include PIC time, cross-country time, turbine time, and EFIS (electronic flight instrument system) time. In this case you will need to bring some form of spreadsheet or other documentation to justify how you derived the flight times entered on your application that are not included in your military flight records.

Skeletons in the Closet

One of the scariest parts about applying for an airline job are those probing questions that you would rather not answer because you're afraid the response you provide will sink your chances of getting hired. Hopefully this section will alleviate your fears because the reality is that most of these concerns exist only in your head. There are very few issues that are truly showstoppers with respect to getting hired by the airlines as long as you're honest and upfront on your application. In this section I will also teach you a technique for minimizing the impact of confessing your sins on the application. Hopefully, you will sleep better at night after reading this section, knowing that your future as an airline pilot is still secure.

We all have them…things in our past that we are not that proud of. The application is going to ask about some of these things; there is no way around it. The key here is *never lie* on an airline application. Most of these sins can be forgiven (except maybe a murder conviction) as long as you disclose them on your application and can tell a good story in the interview about what you learned from the experience. What will not be forgiven, and will certainly cause you to lose the job, is if they discover that you lied about something on your application or tried to hide something.

Some examples of the type of questions that will expose skeletons in the closet include:

- Any traffic violations?
- Any failed check rides?
- Have you ever been disciplined for violating a flight rule?
- Have you ever been caught having sex in public?

Again, the key here is don't lie, but also don't expose something unnecessarily (e.g. "well, no, I was never *caught* having sex in public").

Traffic violations are a skeleton most of us have in the closet. With the exception of a DUI/DWI, most traffic violations should be no problem. Airlineapps.com, used by Delta Air Lines and United Airlines, will ask you to list any traffic infractions including any tickets or accidents. Pilotcredentials.com, used by American Airlines, FedEx, and Southwest Airlines does not ask you to list traffic infractions, but that doesn't mean they won't research your driving record as part of your background check.

Again, don't sweat it too much, we were all teenagers once and therefore most of us have a few tickets and/or accidents on our driving record. This is a very forgivable sin, as long as you confess and don't try to hide it. Even if you can't find a ticket or accident in your driving records (some of these records are expunged after a certain number of years, it varies from state to state), go ahead and list it on your application anyway if you know about it. You might have to estimate some of the details such as date, amount of the fine, or name of state sheriff or city police agency that issued the ticket, but that's better than not listing it and then having it show up on your background check.

Probably the most common skeleton in the closet for pilots is a check ride failure. You might be under the mistaken impression that a failed check ride will automatically eliminate your chances of getting hired. A couple check ride failures are not all that uncommon in a pilot's aviation career. Especially if they happened earlier in your career when you had less airmanship/experience. The airlines know that and generally speaking they're willing to give you the benefit of the doubt.

If you answer yes to a check ride failure question on your application, the application should give you a place to explain the details of your failure. The key here is to take accountability regardless of what you perceive caused the check ride failure. What you don't want to do is blame your failure on someone or something else. A comment such as "my check pilot had a reputation as being hard on new pilots in the squadron" or "the check pilot said I went below MDA but that's because the needle on my altimeter got stuck" is a sure way to eliminate your chances of getting an interview.

Here is an example where you might be able to avoid answering yes and still keep a clean conscience. On the question of check-ride failures, I had originally answered yes on my applications because I had failed my multiengine stage-check rating at Embry-Riddle Aeronautical University (ERAU) early in my aviation career. I just assumed that counted as a check-ride failure. Then I attended a job fair a few months later and sat in on a presentation given by the director of pilot hiring from HR at an airline that I was targeting. He asked if anyone had any questions about the application, and so I asked if my stage-check failure constituted a check-ride failure. His answer surprised me. He said that ERAU is a Part 141 school; therefore, as long as I did not receive a "pink slip" (FAA paperwork documenting a check-ride failure), I did not need to answer yes on the check-ride failure question on the application.

Similarly, most military pilots don't get through UPT unscathed. In air force pilot training, there are between seven and nine phase-check rides in the program depending on which syllabus or track you choose. It is quite common for student pilots to fail one or more of those check rides. Some airlines would want you to answer yes on the check-ride failure question with regards to UPT phase checks, and others will tell you to only include it if the check ride occurred after UPT and is part of your permanent flying record (in the air force, we called that a Form 8 evaluation). The bottom line is play it conservative. Either answer yes or call or e-mail the HR department and ask the question if there is any doubt…but definitely do not lie.

So what do you do about the "skeleton in the closet" questions that have you dead to rights, and you're forced to answer yes to avoid lying on your application? Well, there is a certain art form to confessing your sins on an application. I call it turning a negative into a positive. If you answer yes to these questions, the website will usually ask you to explain the circumstances by allowing you to write a narrative about the event. In the check-ride failure example above, the website will probably direct you to list the date and type of check-ride failure…but don't stop there. Make sure you tell your side of the story and spin it into a positive. For instance, here is the response I provided for my multiengine check-ride failure at ERAU (before I knew I could answer no to this question):

> Multiengine End of Course stage check (Part 141), Embry-Riddle Aeronautical University, May 1994. I have since earned my FAA multiengine certification (and multiengine instructor) and passed every FAA and military check ride attempted (30+ successful check rides)

That sounds like a pretty impressive accomplishment instead of a single failure, doesn't it? OK, now you try it on your skeleton question. See, not all that difficult, is it? I credit my wife, who is a public-relations professional, with teaching me that trick.

Violating flight rules is a little more serious offense. If the application asks if you have ever been disciplined for violating a flight rule and your answer is yes, then your best bet is to throw yourself on the mercy of the court. Admit your sin, and then use the narrative space provided to explain how the experience turned you into a safer, more mature pilot with (hopefully) a flawless safety record since the event in question.

As you can see, a lot of the things you have been stressing about or maybe you were tempted to conveniently "forget" to list on your application are really no big deal. The airline pilot hiring departments have seen thousands of applications and you would be shocked at some of the stories they've heard, and yet, still hired that person. They know that nobody is perfect and they are willing to overlook almost anything as long as you are honest and upfront with it on your application and in the interview. Being deceitful or dishonest is a sure way to lose the interview or the job so **just don't do it!**

Availability Date

I was warned by several friends to be conservative and not list a date earlier than I knew I could start training. I was told that if you got hired and could not start on your listed availability date, you would then lose the job. To be honest, I found that advice to not be exactly true. I ran into several people who interviewed with me who were not available to start training right away because of their military commitment. They explained in the interview that they were trying to get released from their military commitment early, but if the military didn't approve their application for early release, they wouldn't be available to start airline training for up to six months in some cases. To my astonishment, the airline let them get away with this.

In my Delta Air Lines interview, we were told that you can defer training by one class date. In other words, if they call you for a class date, you can tell them you are unavailable the first time they call. However, the next time they call you with a later class date, you are forced to either accept or lose the job offer. Different airlines have different policies; make sure you research for the airlines you are targeting.

It's true that your listed availability date will impact when you get called for an interview. In my experience, most applicants get called for an interview within three to four months of their listed availability date. However, previous guidance still applies...don't lie on an application. If you have a date listed, you need to be able to justify why you listed it. Don't list immediate availability just to get an earlier interview if you know there is no way you can be available until a year from now. That probably won't work out so well for you.

Keep an Application-Tracking Spreadsheet

One last piece of unsolicited advice with respect to airline applications. If you're using the shotgun approach of applying to every airline you would possibly be willing to work for, it can get confusing to keep track of. I recommend creating an "Airline Application Tracker" spreadsheet to track things like the date the application was submitted, the date the application was last updated, the date the résumé was last updated, any applicable notes, and so on. By now you know that I'm all about saving you time and effort, so check www.cockpit2cockpit.com for an "Airline Application Tracker" spreadsheet included in the *Cockpit to Cockpit* Support Package materials.

Summary

Before you submit your first application, don't forget to clean up your social media profile. Don't post anything you wouldn't want an airline-hiring department to see or read. Scrub your social media accounts thoroughly and delete anything that could be questioned by HR.

I know all this application stuff sounds like a pain in the ass, and it is. It will take a lot more time than you think it will. It will go a lot smoother if you gather all your required paperwork (see chapter 5) ahead of time. Even then, expect to spend three to four days on your first application. As you start filling out more applications, it will go faster, but each airline's application process has its own new challenges and frustrations. I've said it already, and I will say it again: **getting a job is a full-time job!**

Well, that's it. You have your applications submitted...let the waiting begin. Hmmmmm, phone's not ringing yet, huh? In the next chapter, we will discuss some things you can do to increase your chances of getting an interview.

THE CHECKLIST

- **Sanitize your online social media image.**
- **Consider joining FAPA and/or The Pilot Network to get quick notification about airline application windows.**
- **Establish a professional e-mail address using a first.last@emailprovider.com format for your airline applications.**
- **Determine your availability date.**
- **Obtain a copy of your most recent military security clearance application to make your airline application process easier.**
- **Create a Microsoft Word document that contains the basic information common to each application such as residential address history, job descriptions, work address history, supervisor names and telephone numbers. Use as a "cut and paste" document for future applications.**
- **Use "keywords" liberally throughout your application and résumé to increase your application computer score.**
- **Check your application for common errors such as unexplained gaps in employment history, address history, inaccurate flight times, etc.**

- **Print and review the application before submitting electronically.**
- **Submit your airline applications approximately one year prior to your availability date.**
- **Edit your e-mail spam filters to ensure your e-mail provider won't flag e-mails from the airline's HR department as spam.**
- **Clean out your e-mail spam folder and check it daily just in case your e-mail filters don't work.**
- **Keep an airline application tracking spreadsheet.**

CHAPTER 7

Increase Your Chances of Getting an Interview

REMEMBER BACK IN chapter 2 when I told you that **getting a job is a full-time job**? Well, here is where you are really going to have to go that extra mile to make sure the outcome of this journey is a successful, smooth transition from military pilot to airline pilot. If you follow the advice in this chapter, you will greatly increase your chances of getting an interview at some if not all of your targeted airlines, assuming your flying background, leadership experience, education, etc. is competitive to begin with.

Attend Some Job Fairs

I know what you're thinking..."I don't need to attend job fairs; the airlines will want me just because I'm a highly skilled military pilot!" You are correct in thinking that the airlines do want highly skilled military pilots. However, if you just rest on your laurels and expect the phone to ring while one thousand of your military pilot friends go to the job fairs and meet with the recruiters in person, guess who has the better chance of getting an interview?

Making the effort to attend a job fair shows the airline that you are serious and motivated about working for their company. The fact that you were willing to spend your hard-earned money and time to travel across the country and wait in line for up to an hour just for three to five minutes of face time with their recruiters will be noticed by the airline hiring department.

I attended a job fair in 2014 and I was fortunate enough to meet with the senior manager for pilot hiring programs at United Airlines. He provided me some advice about how to maximize the points available for LORs on the United Airlines' application. I followed his advice and within weeks of making the suggested changes, I got a call from United Airlines. This stuff really works! He also told me that over 60 percent of United Airlines' pilot interviews come from people they meet at job fairs.

The pilot job fair scene has changed quite a bit since *Cockpit to Cockpit* first edition was released. Many of the major airlines have announced that 2017 will be the last year that they will be attending the traditional job fairs. Instead, each airline will host their own in-house pilot recruiting events at their company headquarters.

The traditional large and widely attended pilot job fairs are hosted annually by professional organizations that seek to promote minority recruitment into the aerospace industry. These organizations include Women in Aviation International (WAI) www.wai.org, Organization of Black Aerospace Professionals (OBAP) www.obap.org, and the National Gay Pilots Association (NGPA) www.ngpa.org. You don't have to be a minority to attend these job fairs; they are open to anyone interested in aviation. In addition to hosting a pilot job fair, these events also offer some amazing guest speakers and great educational seminars including classes on résumé writing skills and interview skills.

In the past, the major airlines attended these large job fairs and pilots would wait in long lines for a chance to meet one-on-one with airline recruiters. The long lines were a detractor to many pilots. Another detractor was the cost of admission, in some cases exceeding $400. The upside of the traditional pilot job fairs is that they are opened to anyone willing to pay the cost of admission. However, since most major airlines will no longer be attending the traditional job fairs for the purpose of pilot recruiting starting in 2018, I foresee the attendance at these events dropping off dramatically in the near future.

FAPA hosts several smaller job fairs throughout the year. In the past, FAPA-hosted job fairs usually featured at least one major airline as well as many of the regional air carriers. FAPA provides a members-only line at their job fairs that gets you through the lines faster. They also provide excellent interview-preparation services. You can get more information by visiting their website at www.fapa.aero. Aero Crew Solutions is a similar service that sometimes hosts job fairs also. Given the major airlines' recent trend toward in-house pilot recruiting events, I doubt they will attend future small job fairs, however, it is likely these events will still attract regional air carriers, foreign airlines, and possibly some of the cargo air carriers.

Recently, the major airlines began hosting their own in-house pilot recruiting events. There is no cost to attend these events but, unlike the traditional pilot job fairs, these events are small, often limited to just a few hundred pilots. It's a more intimate experience where those lucky enough to get an invite will get to spend more time with the recruiters, take a tour of the facilities, and interact with many HR and other airline personnel. Most airlines will require that you have an application submitted as a prerequisite to being invited. Each airline uses a different system to determine who will be invited. Some of these events are military and/or veteran only events. Some airlines announce a date and time that the registration window will open, and the slots are gone in a matter of minutes (may the fastest internet connection win). Some airlines will only send invites to those who meet their selection criteria but the airline may or may not announce what those criteria are.

As a business owner whose business is to help you get hired by the airlines, I track the hiring trends pretty closely. I have observed a trend since the airlines began hosting pilot-recruiting events. It appears the majority of pilots who attend a pilot-recruiting event do get an interview invite within the next year. If you are lucky enough to have a chance to attend one of these recruiting events, don't pass it up.

So how do you find out about these pilot recruiting events? The airline will usually announce it on their company website under the "Careers" or "Work Here" link. Sometimes they announce on social media sites such as Facebook or Twitter so make sure you "like" or "follow" the airlines you're targeting. Probably the best way to hear about them is through the "pilot grapevine" also knows as The Pilot Network group on Facebook. You will recall from chapter 6 that Delta uses their own Delta Air Lines Pilot Recruiting Facebook group and American Airlines uses their American Airlines Talent Runway website for advertising pilot recruiting events.

JetBlue also hosts an annual pilot recruiting event called Vets In Blue (VIB). JetBlue is a very veteran-friendly company. VIB is specifically intended to offer veterans (that's you) a fast-track ticket to employment with JetBlue. The company invites a select number of veterans (roughly a few hundred) to visit the company headquarters in New York City to see what JetBlue is all about and convince you to come fly for them. Just by attending the VIB, you are almost 100 percent guaranteed an interview within the next year. The VIB program takes place in November (to coincide with Veterans Day). Sometimes they will host another VIB event in the spring-time also depending on how many pilots they need to hire that year. Sounds great, right, so what's the catch? The catch is they don't advertise VIB in the traditional sense, and you have to be invited. Make sure you check the veteran box on your application. JetBlue also sends out an internal company e-mail to advertise upcoming VIB events to its pilots. The other way to get invited is to know someone at JetBlue who will send you the e-mail invite with the details.

If you plan to attend a job fair or pilot-recruiting event, there are a few things you should know before you go. The first is what to wear. I will cover men's dress code first. If you have not already done so, it's time to go buy a nice interview suit. I recommend waiting until Men's Warehouse or Joseph A. Banks has one of their "Buy one, get two free" sales. You will want more than one suit, since some airline interviews are a two-day process (Delta, American, and FedEx). Stay conservative, generally a dark-gray or dark-blue suit with a white shirt. If you really want to impress, buy a tie that matches the logo colors of the airline you are meeting with. Does it really matter to them what color tie you wear? Probably not, but you want to convey that you came all this way just to meet with their airline because ever since you were a little boy, you dreamed of working for XYZ airline. Make sure you have a fresh haircut, polished shoes, trimmed nails, freshly shaved face, you get the point.

If the event is advertised as business casual, then a nice pair of slacks or khakis with a sports coat and oxford shirt without tie will work. Keeping conservative is still the rule of the day. Yes, you can get away without the sports coat with or without a tie if you want to. You can also take it up a notch and wear a suit with no tie. Don't wear jeans, even with a nice shirt that's a bit too casual.

For the ladies, most of the same rules apply. You will want two or three conservative, dark-colored pants suits or skirt suits. This advice comes from my wife who is a public relations expert. She advises businesswomen on attire, including members of Congress. Her recommendation is to avoid the tight fitting suits at all costs. Instead, opt for the most flattering tailoring possible, avoiding gaps or pulling. As for the makeup, keep it neutral and professional. She strongly advises the "fresh-face ladies" to at least wear some mascara, slightly colored lip-gloss, and a light dusting of powder. If you don't normally wear makeup, try it on for a few days before the event to be sure it doesn't flake or spread out too much. At the event, reapply powder and lip-gloss every time you take a restroom break to avoid late-day shine. For jewelry, again stay conservative. Consider bringing a colored silk accent scarf to achieve the same effect as the men's tie choice mentioned above.

Women's business casual leaves a wide array of fashions that could fit the bill. Again, skewing conservative keeps you on the safe side. That said, my wife and I discussed this at length and she considers this to be a fashion danger-zone for women.

The most important element for women in business casual is to look polished, totally pulled together with everything fitting properly. You want to limit the amount of skin showing (remember these are her words, not mine). Save your physical assets for the gym and the beach. As tempting as sleeveless may be, it is not recommended unless you wear a sweater over the top and leave it on the whole day.

Business casual for women does not mean khakis and a polo shirt. Currently the wrap dress or single piece business dress is a strong option that is comfortable and looks good with mid and low heels or flats. She recommends staying with mid heels or kitten heels over flats if at all possible. If winter weather is an issue, attractive low boots are also an option. Make an investment in an oversized purse or stylized bag that can hold folders and touch-up makeup. Do not use a tote bag, even if provided by the event. Instead, break it down and place the items inside your purse. This helps to maintain the polished look you are trying to achieve. Although less fashion forward, flattering dress slacks with an Oxford style blouse or shirt works well and is great with flats. Mind the gapping on dresses, blouses, and shirts. Bring extra safety pins in your purse for back up. Make sure the heels on your shoes are new or have been replaced recently. Nobody wants to hear a bare nail clicking on the floor (the same advice could be given for the soles of men's shoes). A thin cardigan sweater kept in a Ziploc in your purse is a good idea in case the room is cold.

For both the interview and business casual pilot recruiting events, make sure to paint your nails clear or get a manicure within a day before the event. Ideally have the manicure done using a nail polish that you own and can bring with you if needed for touch-ups. A great hint is to have a cuticle oil stick in your purse. Make sure to clean your conservative jewelry the day before the event.

You will be amazed at what some people wear to these job fairs. I have seen cowboy boots, shiny reflective suits, purple suits, short skirts on women, you name it. Don't be that pilot. Just keep it conservative; you can make an impression with your radiant personality. I have also seen military folks wearing their dress uniforms. I don't recommend that either…it says, "Hi, I'm the military guy/girl who can't let it go and I'll never fit into your organizational culture."

It is a little bit humorous when you show up to these events and see hundreds of other pilots dressed just like you. You will feel like a penguin on an iceberg as you waddle around with your folder full of résumés waiting to meet with an airline recruiter. So how do you differentiate yourself and make enough of an impression that you convince them to give your application a look? That is your goal here, to make enough of a positive impression that they decide to pull your application and score it, hopefully resulting in an interview invite. Well, here are a few tips that will increase your chances. You already did the first thing: you showed up looking professional. You just jumped ahead of 10–15 percent of the competition that did not follow that cardinal rule.

Another easy differentiator is high-quality résumé paper. It astounds me how many people show up to job fairs with résumés printed on plain white copy paper. Spend the $15 and go to Office Depot and buy a couple packs of the professional linen ivory or beige résumé paper. *Boom*, you just made a better impression than 70 percent of your peers. When you print your résumés on professional résumé paper, make sure the watermark is right side up (it's a small detail that's easy to miss) by holding it up to a window (daytime) or light in the room. Make sure you bring plenty of résumé copies. If it's a major job fair attended by many airlines, bring about twenty to thirty copies to be safe. If it's a pilot-recruiting event at a major airline, bring about ten to twenty copies; you will likely speak with multiple recruiters and HR personnel throughout the day.

Here is a technique that will really help you stand out from the crowd. The airline recruiter expects you to show up with a nice résumé. However, they are not expecting, but should be pleasantly surprised, if you show up with a few (three to five) recommendation letters in addition to your résumé. As a suggestion, I wouldn't just hand them over with your résumé. Instead try this, when asked for your résumé just say, "Here is my résumé, do you mind if I also provide you with a few recommendation letters from my friends and co-workers who work here?". Now pause, and wait for the tears of joy to start flowing as you hand them a tissue. Have several sets of LORs ready to go, one set for each résumé you hand out.

I used this technique when I attended a JetBlue VIB event in 2014 at the company headquarters in New York. I spoke with half a dozen JetBlue pilots and HR personnel during the event and I gave each a copy of my résumé and packet of five LORs. I received an interview invite phone call before I had even left New York to travel home the next day.

You have probably invested hundreds of dollars in travel costs to attend these pilot-recruiting events, so make sure you make it worthwhile...*do your homework*. Research the airline and make sure you can talk intelligently about why you want to work there. I did my research before departing home and made a cheat sheet page of notes about the company that I could study while traveling to the event or while waiting in line.

You should know their core values and make sure you give them examples of how you exemplify those values. The company website "About XYZ Airline" link, usually located at the bottom of the homepage, is a great place to find this information. If not there, ask anyone you know who works at that airline. You should know a basic summary of the airline's history. You don't have to be able to recite every detail of their timeline; just have a good idea of the company's beginnings and major milestones along the way. You should also have a good idea about the basic company fact sheet, including domicile locations, fleet size, type of aircraft, recent awards, and so on.

Lastly, you should research and be able to discuss current events at XYZ airline. A great place to find out what's going on with that airline is from their press releases. There will be a "Press Room" or "Media Kit" link either near the "About XYZ Airline" link or possibly within that link.

Although a pilot-recruiting event is not an interview, you should treat it as such. Be prepared with a brief (no more than one-to-two-minute) response to the question "Tell me about yourself." Don't just regurgitate your résumé; they have that information in their hands. Sure, you need to hit the highlights, but also give them some personal information that helps them relate to you, such as "...and I just celebrated my tenth wedding anniversary on a Disney cruise with my beautiful wife, Megan, and our three kids, Cody, Trevor, and Sue Ellen." Chances are the interviewer can relate to being married, having kids, or having a weird attraction to Minnie Mouse. Other questions to be ready for include:

"Why do you want to work here?"
"Why should we hire you?"
"What do you know about XYZ airline?"

Another key to success at the job fair is to keep the conversation flowing. If there is an awkward silence in your face time with the recruiter, you will probably see them quickly wrap it up, and he or she will be on to the next candidate. A good way to keep the conversation flowing is to come prepared with your own questions about that airline. As the end of your time with them approaches, they will probably ask you if you have any questions for them. That's your warning sign that you are about to lose their attention and end the session. You probably do have a lot of questions about that airline, so don't be afraid to ask a few. It can be anything from questions about the interview process to future growth plans for the airline. On the flip side, you don't want the session to go so long that you become the annoying kid who won't go away. Keep a good read on the interviewer's mannerisms and body language. If you sense the interviewer getting antsy, help him or her wrap it up in a non-awkward way, and you're on to the next line.

Here is the biggest differentiator that you can use to stand out from the other penguins. As the face-time session comes to a close, ask recruiters if you can get their business card in case you think of any more questions. On that business card is usually a mailing address or at least an e-mail address. A quick thank-you e-mail followed up by a handwritten thank-you card goes a long way! I would guess only 2–3 percent of job fair attendees use this tactic. It really shows a warm personal touch that makes the recruiter think, "Geez, what a great guy/gal. That's exactly the type of person we need working here at XYZ airlines. Let me go pull their application and try to get them an interview."

Should I Get a Type Rating?

Certainly having a type rating on your ATP looks better than not having one. However, type ratings are extremely expensive ($7000-plus depending on the type of aircraft you're getting typed in and that's in addition to the costs for an ATP-CTP course). A type rating is generally required by the FAA to act as PIC or SIC of an aircraft requiring two or more flight crewmembers and/or weighing more than 12,500 pounds. In the Part 121 air-carrier world, the B-737 is considered the entry-level type rating and is the one most commonly obtained for military pilots transitioning to the airlines. Type ratings are accomplished via simulator training. So do you need to get a type rating or not? It depends on the current status of hiring in the industry.

When hiring is slow and there are more qualified applicants available in the "hiring pool" than the number of cockpits that need to be filled, then the airlines are more selective about candidate qualifications. In that scenario, a type rating can be the difference between getting an interview and not. Southwest Airlines historically required its pilot applicants to possess a B-737 type rating for two reasons. The first is that it saved the company a lot of dinero (that means money for you non-French-speaking types). Southwest could provide less in-house training if they hired pilots who already had a B-737 type rating. The second reason is it demonstrated a high degree of motivation and commitment of loyalty to Southwest Airlines from the applicant. If applicants were willing to spend $5000 to $10,000 for a B-737 type rating, they were far less likely to leave Southwest Airlines for another company after being hired and trained.

Recently, Southwest has dropped their application requirement to possess a B-737 type rating, because the hiring pool of qualified pilots is rapidly shrinking. Hiring has been at all-time highs in the past year and is forecast to continue that way for another decade at least. Southwest has now fallen in line with the rest of the airline industry, meaning that at the time this book was written, all airlines including Southwest will provide you with the required type rating as part of your initial qualification training at no cost to you (reference the earlier discussion about training commitments in chapter 4). That being said, an otherwise equally qualified applicant with a B-737 type rating is far more likely to get an interview at Southwest Airlines (or any airline for that matter) than an applicant without one.

Despite what you may have heard, getting a B-737 type rating will not hurt (and will actually help) your chances of getting hired at airlines other than Southwest Airlines. Yes, they might give you a little grief in the interview with a question such as "I see you have a B-737 type rating; I guess your interview over at Southwest didn't work out, huh?" All they are doing is gauging how serious you are about committing to their airline. They want to know you're not going to leave them for Southwest. If you get that type of question in the interview, you just need to tell them that getting a type rating was the next logical step in continuing your professional aviation career as you transition from military to airline pilot, and then launch into your reasons why you really want to work for XYZ airlines. The fact is, having a type rating makes you a more attractive candidate and gives you a leg up on your peers.

We discussed earlier that checking as many boxes as possible on the application adds points to your application computer score. Having a type rating will allow you to check another box and add some points. It also gives you some training in the civilian flying world, and more specifically in the Part 121 world that you will be working in at any airline. Airlines logically prefer candidates with type ratings because it shows the candidates are serious about furthering their professional aviation knowledge and skill set.

Another consideration to think about when deciding if you want to pursue a type rating is that you can combine your ATP and type-rating training into one program. If you don't already have an ATP, doing it in conjunction with a type rating is a way (albeit a more expensive way) to kill two birds with one stone. If you are worried about the cost, read on, my friend...help is on the way.

Most of you probably stopped reading this section a few paragraphs back when I told you that a type rating could cost more than $7000. However, in case you're still with me on this topic, there is a silver lining to this cloud. It's called the GI Bill. As military officers, most of you are eligible to use the GI Bill to pay for advanced college education or professional training for yourself or your dependents. So, as long as you don't care about your spouse or children's education, you can use it for your type rating instead. But seriously, it's worth a trip to your base education office to get more details about the GI Bill and determine what is the best use of this amazing resource for you and your family. **Warning:** make sure you ask them about any additional service commitment incurred by using the GI Bill.

Depending on where you take your training, most schools and aviation-training companies will accept the GI Bill as a form of payment for a type rating. When I used the GI Bill to pay for my B-737 type rating in 2014, the GI Bill offered up to $11,000 per year for up to four years. That should allow you to use one year's worth for your type rating and still have three years' worth of benefits left for your dependents. Again, check with your base education office to get details about using your GI Bill benefits.

Networking Still Works

As we discussed earlier, when the major airlines began hiring again in October 2013, they were flooded with over ten thousand applications each. They needed some way to sort through the stack and get to the most qualified applications. It was about that time when the major airlines transitioned to computer-application scoring. Many chief pilots, HR department leaders, vice presidents (VP) of flight operations, and other airline leadership personnel would tell you they have no control over who gets an interview and who does not. They will lead you to believe that's it's all done by the computer screening. I'm throwing the bullshit flag on that one.

I have plenty of friends who "coincidentally" received an interview invitation within a week of having an airline buddy (usually a very senior airline buddy) hand walk a copy of their résumé into the chief pilot's office. Trust me; networking works! That doesn't necessarily mean that every applicant who has a friend go to bat for them with airline leadership is going to get an interview, but it drastically increases the chances of having your résumé and application pulled out of the stack to be scored. If your score meets the airline's magic threshold, you will most likely get an interview out of it.

You need to do whatever it takes to get your résumé in front of a senior decision maker within the airline. During my transition I had an American Airlines friend invite myself and five other pilots to the American Airlines company picnic. Of course, we all brought copies of our résumés. During the picnic my friend introduced us to the VP of flight operations who asked us if we were all trying to get hired at American. After chatting with us for a few minutes, the VP of flight operations told my American Airlines friend to drop copies of our résumés on his desk. Half of us received interview invites within the next month.

In October 2013, Delta Airlines released an internal memo about pilot hiring. In that memo, Delta outlined the detailed process they would use for selecting pilot applicants for interviews. Internal recommendations were highly encouraged, as was a personal e-mail to the pilot-selection team. Several of my friends who fly for Delta have told me that the pilot-selection team will pull and score any application that receives an internal e-mail recommendation. My apologies to Delta pilots everywhere who are about to be inundated with requests to e-mail the pilot-selection team on behalf of the requestor based on my advice.

So what if you don't have any close friends who work in the airlines? First, I would tell you that you screwed up throughout your time in the military by not keeping in touch with coworkers who got out and went to the airlines before you did. But then I would tell you that you can still make airline contacts just by networking when you fly commercial. Every time you take an airline trip, dress smart casual and chat up the flight attendants and pilots at every opportunity.

Let them know you're applying to that airline and ask for advice. Most will be more than willing to help. It's also a good idea to keep an electronic copy of your résumé stored on your smartphone. If the opportunity presents itself, ask if you can send them your résumé. You never know whom they might share it with within the company.

You may encounter some formal networking opportunities where an airline representative can't accept your résumé due to legal reasons (you would be surprised how much power the lawyers have in the airline industry). As an example, an airline that is attending a military/veteran hiring event is legally not allowed to accept résumés unless they are also conducting interviews at the event. It has to do with federal government regulations regarding veteran hiring practices, but that's not important right now. If you find yourself in this situation, you need some other kind of "leave behind" product that allows your new contact to remember you. The average pilot in transition would be stumped in this situation, but not you, you're a *Cockpit to Cockpit* reader who realizes that **getting a job is a full time job**; you will be ready to whip out your handy dandy new business card designed just for the occasion!

A business card is a great way to give someone your essential information if they can't take your résumé. If you make a great first impression and hand them a business card, it's quite possible they will get your information to the hiring department and get your application scored. Business cards can be relatively inexpensive (roughly $30 for 250 count) and you can create your own design and order online using www.vistaprint.com or numerous competitors. You can either use your current military job title, or use the more generic title of "Professional Pilot." Include your pertinent contact information and list the highlights of your aviation certificates, qualifications, aircraft flown, and a round number of your most impressive flight times (i.e. "2500+ TT, 1700+ PIC). Most importantly, you should provide a link to your LinkedIn profile and make sure that profile looks awesome! You can look at my LinkedIn page www.linkedin.com/in/marc-himelhoch to generate some ideas for improving your LinkedIn profile.

I had a great networking opportunity fall right into my lap on my way to a job fair in Las Vegas. I was specifically going to that particular job fair to meet with Southwest Airlines. I flew Southwest on my way there, and I happened to be reading a copy of the book *Nuts*, a book about the history and unique culture of Southwest Airlines, during the flight. The woman sitting next to me noticed what I was reading and asked if I was interested in Southwest Airlines. I told her I was an air force pilot on my way to a job fair to try to get hired by Southwest. Turns out she (and everyone sitting around me) was a Southwest Airlines employee and a member of the Southwest Airlines Culture Committee on their way to their annual Culture Committee meeting. They spent the rest of the flight giving me great advice and encouragement, and they all signed my book. I was able to exchange contact information with my seat-mate and new contact at Southwest Airlines. It made for a great icebreaker the next day when I met with the Southwest recruiter and told him how much I had enjoyed meeting the Culture Committee and how their positive energy reinforced my desire to work for such a great company.

As mentioned earlier, The Pilot Network (TPN) is a tremendous networking resource for pilots. Joining is just a simple matter of sending a request to the group administrator via their Facebook page so he can verify you are a pilot. A couple of military pilots created TPN for the specific purpose of helping other pilots network. There are many airline pilots active in the group, and you can ask them specific questions about their airlines and also get great advice about getting hired. The questions you have are the probably the same questions thousands of others have and the daily discussion threads on TPN will most likely contain answers to those questions. They also have a great smartphone app. The Pilot Network also maintains a website located at www.thepilotnetwork.org. Additionally, TPN puts out a very informative quarterly newsletter, as well as podcasts that include interviews with industry experts and cover topics relevant to any aspiring pilot looking to further his or her aviation career.

Update Your Application and Résumé Frequently

I have heard from various sources that airlines track how often you update your application and résumé as a measure of your work ethic and how motivated you are to work there. Some of my friends swear that they didn't get an interview invite until they started making several updates per week. I don't know how true that is, but it can't hurt, right? According to Keith Steele, owner of Centerline Interview Consulting, one major airline had 15,000 applications on file in 2016, but only 5,000 of those had been updated in the past three months!

Not all airline websites will allow you to make changes after initial submission, but if you can make updates, you should do so frequently. For one thing, it makes sense to me that in this digital age, the longer an application sits dormant, the more likely it is to get kicked out of the system to make room for fresh applications.

Another reason for frequent updates is that you have the opportunity to improve your application score. As you build more flight time, gain new duty titles, garner new awards, and so on, you obviously want to add those things to enhance your application. Be sure to update your résumé (if applicable) at the same time when you update your application. This is one of those "attention to detail" items. For instance, if you add some flight hours to your application, you should update the flight hours on your résumé also and upload the latest version as an attachment to your application. Overkill? Maybe...but going the extra mile is usually a good thing in the eyes of the airline.

If you aren't actively flying, it may not be quite as easy to find things to update. Just go in there and change "happy" to "glad" periodically so the computer system will register a log-in and update. The Southwest Airlines pilot hiring manager stated at the OBAP 2017 convention that you should update your Southwest Airlines application at least monthly. He said even just entering your availability date again and hitting save will record an update.

Use Social Media

One last advantage you can give yourself is to be an active supporter of XYZ airline on social media. Every airline these days has a social-media presence, and their marketing departments actively track both positive and negative social-media posts as well as who their loyal patrons are. You want to be one of those loyal patrons. Join the frequent-flier programs for the airlines you are targeting. Follow them on Twitter; "Like" their Facebook page. Throw some positive comments on their social-media posts, and make some positive tweets.

As I mentioned earlier, some of the major airlines use social media to announce their hiring windows and pilot-recruiting events. Ask on TPN to find out if an airline has a specific pilot hiring social media site, some do.

Why Am I Not Getting Any Interviews?

If you have a solid flying background, follow the advice given in this book, and are a generally good person whom people like, then your phone should be ringing off the hook with interview invites when you are three to six months away from your given availability date. Remember, you are competing with a large number of highly qualified military and civilian pilots for a limited number of interview slots. The HR folks are looking for candidates who go the extra mile and show a high degree of motivation and enthusiasm to work at their airline. You want to be that Johnny go-getter!

If you have not received an interview invite by the time of your date available listed on your applications, something is wrong. It's probably one of five reasons: your application or résumé work was sloppy, your reputation preceded you, your flying credentials are not competitive, you need more LORs, or in the case of American Airlines, you didn't test well on the OFA (the personality screening) portion of the application. It's also possible that the airline you are targeting may have slowed their hiring pace due to a log jam in their available training slots…all you can do about that is be patient or apply to other airlines.

The first one is an easy fix. Print out your application and résumé and go over them with a fine-tooth comb looking for spelling and grammar errors. Better yet, give them to a friend or coworker and ask them to go over it with a fine-tooth comb (a six-pack will generally be all that is required for said services). Next, go back and read this book again. Did you really follow all the advice, or did you think some of it was unnecessary? Are there places you could sprinkle some more keywords in the application? Are there unexplained gaps in your employment history or residential timeline? You may want to ask your interview-preparation service to look over your application and résumé too.

They have lots of experience in this department and may be able to spot some errors the untrained eye might miss.

If you really want to cover your bases, you can hire the professional application and résumé review service Checked And Set, www.checkedandset.net. The owner, Captain Charlie Venema, is a B-787 Captain and former pilot hiring board member at a major airline. He has a team of experts who know exactly what to look for. Checked And Set also offers airline job fair preparation sessions. Disclaimer: I have not personally used Checked And Set but they are highly recommended on TPN.

Another possibility is that somewhere during your military career, you made an enemy (knowingly or unknowingly) who now works at that airline. That person may be dragging your name through the mud to the airline's pilot-hiring department. This scenario could happen at one airline, but it's unlikely to happen at all the airlines you have applied to unless you were a complete asshole during your time in the military. For the record, I don't think that's the case. Even if it were true, most airlines will interview candidates first and won't research you via their pilot workforce until after they have had a chance to meet you in person at the interview.

If you're fairly certain that someone who works at the airline is preventing you from getting an interview, there is something you can do about it; tell your side of the story. Write a letter explaining the conflict and how you dealt with it. Upload it as an attachment to your application. Better yet, ask other pilot friends who work for the airline to go to bat for you by speaking with the chief pilot or pilot hiring manager in HR to back up your side of the story and talk about what a great person you really are.

It might be that your flying experience is just not competitive. Even though you might meet the minimums listed on the company website, you may be suffering in comparison to the competition. Take a hard look at the trip reports and flying experience of those who have interviewed recently at each airline you are targeting. How does your experience stack up? Usually the problem is not enough turbine or PIC time, or maybe you have not been actively flying for the past few years because the military assigned you to a desk. If that's the case, you might need to apply to a regional air carrier (or stay on active duty) or cargo carrier and spend a couple years building up your flight time.

Even if it's just right-seat SIC time, the major airlines look favorably on regional-air-carrier experience, because it is turbine time and you are gaining Part 121 experience. However, if it's PIC time you need, you won't get that at a regional-air-carrier until you upgrade to captain. It will likely take between eighteen and twenty-four months before you can upgrade to captain at most regional carriers. The good news is, many of the regional-air-carriers are offering signing bonuses to offset the lower pay scale, and some of them offer guaranteed interviews with their associated legacy air carrier after a certain period of time.

Additionally, some of the major airlines are now hiring pilots with zero turbine PIC time. The average pilot flight time experience of new hire pilots tends to change based on FAA rule changes and the number of qualified applicants available. It has been rumored that the FAA is currently working on an exemption for military pilots to the ATP 1500 flight hours rule. Keep your eyes and ears out for that in the near future.

If you need to, or choose to, fly for a regional or smaller cargo air carrier to enhance your flying experience, be careful about getting to comfortable in that role regardless of which seat you occupy. I have a theory, with absolutely no empirical evidence to back it up (at least I'm honest), that too much time at a regional or smaller cargo air carrier can actually hurt your chances of getting hired by a major airline. I'm basing this theory purely on personal observations over the past several years after attending many job fairs, meeting many pilots in that scenario, and reading multiple online-posts from various aviation networking sites.

I have observed that some (not all) military pilots who have many years and thousands of hours of flight time with a regional or smaller cargo air carrier seem to have a hard time getting interviews and/or getting hired by the majors. My theory is that the pilot hiring departments at the major airlines consider it odd that an otherwise highly qualified military pilot would want to spend so much time at a regional or smaller cargo airline. Essentially they may think you are damaged goods. They want to see a logical aviation career progression so strive for upgrades, leadership positions, and additional qualifications at every opportunity. If you need to go that route for currency or additional flight time experience, make sure you keep your applications with the majors updated at the same time. Your goal is to minimize the amount of time spent using the regional/cargo carrier as a stepping-stone in your aviation career.

If you have the time and funds, you might also consider obtaining your CFII rating or adding a type rating (B-737 being the most common) to your ATP certificate. Recall from chapter 7 that every box you can check on the application will add points to your application. A B-737 type rating will likely add many points.

The major airlines each have different policies and procedures when it comes to LORs (reference chapter 5). If you're not getting noticed by the airline(s) you have targeted, consider adding some LORs to your application. Even if the airline advertises that they won't read them until after you interview, some airlines do add points to your application for each LOR received, up to a certain maximum number of LORs. Recall from chapter 5 that United Airlines will give you maximum points available for LORs after four "quality" LORs.

In addition to the advice provided here, I'll also recommend you read a great two-part article written by Jason Depew on www.aviationbull.com titled "*Getting Your Airline App Noticed*." He covers some of the same advice I've provided, but he also has some other great ideas to help you out.

Summary

Hopefully this chapter has convinced you that going the extra mile will greatly increase your chances of scoring an interview at your top airline choices. While some of the advice contained in this chapter may not work for you, it definitely won't *decrease* your chances of getting an interview, so you have nothing to lose by trying it. If you aren't getting any calls after a reasonable amount of time, carefully analyze what you think might be causing the problem. Consider using a professional service to review your products and help give you a boost.

Because I'm 100 percent confident that reading this book *will* get you an interview, I'm going to spend chapter 8 discussing various airline interview formats and how you can best prepare for your inevitable interview(s).

THE CHECKLIST

- **Try to attend airline sponsored pilot recruiting events/job fairs for face time with recruiters from your targeted airline(s).**
- **Print your résumés on professional résumé paper.**
- **Bring copies of your LORs to the pilot recruiting events/job fairs in addition to your résumé.**
- **Research the airlines you are targeting so you can ask intelligent questions at recruiting events.**
- **Ask for contact information from the recruiter and follow up with a thank-you note or e-mail.**
- **Consider obtaining a B-737 type rating.**
- **Network with friends and coworkers who are airline pilots or airline employees.**
- **Join The Pilot Network Facebook group and website.**
- **Make frequent updates to your applications.**
- **Follow your targeted airlines on social media and consider becoming a member of their frequent-flier program(s).**

- **Create a LinkedIn profile if you don't already have one.**
- **Create a business card with a link to your LinkedIn profile.**

If you are not receiving any interview invitations:

- **Review your résumé and application for gross errors. Consider using a professional résumé and application review service.**
- **Read this book again in detail; don't just skim it.**
- **Try adding more LORs to your application (except United).**
- **Consider the possibility that you may need to apply to a regional airline (or stay on active duty) to enhance your flying credentials.**
- **If you know someone at the company is talking bad about you, consider writing a letter to tell your side of the story and attach it to your application.**
- **Consider obtaining your CFII, MEI, glider, tail wheel, or other FAA ratings.**

CHAPTER 8

Preparing for the Interview

You've been working really hard to make a successful transition from a military cockpit to an airline cockpit. You read this book, followed all the advice, cleaned up your logbook, built a beautiful résumé, gathered all your required paperwork, toiled for hours filling out applications, went to a couple job fairs, and bought brand-new interview suits. Well, guess what? All that is for *naught* if you blow the interview!

Please don't think that just because you are a highly skilled military aviator with thousands of hours of jet time and a chest full of combat medals that the interview process is just a formality. Of course they are going to hire you, right? Wrong. I know plenty of great military pilots and officers (myself included) who have blown the interview because they didn't effectively prepare.

In this chapter we will discuss the various interview formats used by different airlines. I will suggest common resources you can use to help prepare for each different format. I will also provide you a brief overview of the interview process used at several of the major airline brands.

HR Panel Interview

All airlines will include the HR panel interview as part of their interview process. This is usually considered "the main event." Generally you will meet with two or three interviewers including at least one pilot and one HR representative. Some airlines will break this up into two separate interviews, one with pilot interviewers and another with HR interviewers. The panel interview usually lasts between thirty and forty-five minutes.

You can't start too early in polishing your panel-interview skills. There are some great interview-preparation services out there, and **I can't emphasize enough how important it is to invest in an interview-preparation service**. Yes, it will cost you a few hundred dollars, but it's money well spent considering they are preparing you to get hired into a job where you stand to make several million dollars over the course of your airline career.

Words of caution here, some airline-pilot hiring departments have recently expressed concern about applicants who used interview-preparation services. They genuinely want to know the "real you." In my opinion, you can use an interview-preparation service and still show them the "real you." Of course, you're going to use real stories that actually happened to you. The interview-preparation service can't give you your stories (if they do, they are not a very good service to use); they just teach you how to present your own stories in a way that ensures you accurately and effectively communicate your message as you intended it.

At the OBAP 2017 convention, the Southwest Airlines pilot hiring manager stated that in his experience and in speaking with his peers in the other major airline pilot hiring departments, "ninety percent of pilot interview candidates don't need interview preparation, for the other ten percent it may be appropriate." He went on to say that "the best way to *not get hired* at Southwest Airlines is to not be yourself in the interview."

I'm not trying to scare you out of attending an interview preparation class, in fact I found it quite valuable to my success. However, I would be doing you an injustice if I didn't let you know how the airlines feel about it. If they ask you in the interview if you used a preparation service, it's OK to be honest. They hire candidates every day that *did* use an interview preparation service. However, if you get that question in an interview, it should send up a red flag in your mind because what they may really be warning you with that question is "we perceive you're giving us canned responses and if you don't loosen up and be yourself, you may fail this interview."

While I respect the opinion of the airline pilot hiring managers, I think they've seen too many interview candidates who attended interview-preparation courses but did not properly apply what they learned or perhaps used a sub-par interview preparation service that didn't properly prepare them. You don't want to have canned answers memorized; a good interview- preparation service will tell you the same thing. Memorized stories are not the real you. There is a way to tell your story with all your unique charisma and detail the interviewer is looking for, while simultaneously delivering it in an organized, succinct manner. That is why you take an interview- preparation class.

Emerald Coast Interview Consulting is an interview-preparation service with a stellar reputation among military and civilian pilots alike. They offer online seminars, or you can attend one of their many live seminars hosted at various locations throughout the country. Aaron "Albie" Hagan, president and founder of Emerald Coast, is a former USAF F-15 IP and current FedEx B-767 captain. Albie has a very experienced team with many years of interview-consulting experience. In addition to preparing you for the HR interview, Emerald Coast also provides outstanding preparation for the Line Oriented Interview (LOI) used by Southwest Airlines and FedEx. One of the best deals about using Emerald Coast is that once you have attended their course the first time, you can return as many times as you like for free. I found that I received some of the best value for my money by working with his team members in one-on-one mock-interview sessions during repeat visits. You can check out Emerald Coast for yourself at www.emeraldcoastinterviewconsulting.com.

Another highly recommended interview-preparation service is FAPA. Judy Tarver, vice president, has many years of experience in pilot hiring as part of the HR team at a major airline. Judy and her team have a great track record of successfully helping military pilots prepare for airline interviews. In addition to their interview-preparation service, FAPA hosts airline job fairs and provides financial consulting for current and future airline pilots. The FAPA website, www.fapa.aero, is among the best I have found in researching airline pay scales and other pertinent airline-specific information that is useful in rank ordering your airline dream sheet. FAPA has a great network with various airline HR departments that allows them to provide their members current intelligence on hiring trends and notifications when hiring windows open.

Having worked with both Emerald Coast and FAPA, I highly recommend using either one as they are both excellent at what they do. Centerline Interview Consulting is another interview preparation service that is popular among pilots. Centerline counselors all have pilot hiring interview team experience. They use a very personally-tailored process to work with you from the moment you sign up until you're hired including application and résumé review. You can check out their website at www.centerlineinterviewprep.com.

I have also heard good things on TPN about Cage Marshall Consulting. Cage Marshall has been in the business for decades; they are one of the most experienced interview-consulting firms in the industry. For more information visit www.cageconsulting.com

Another option is Career Takeoff, www.careertakeoff.com. The owner of Career Takeoff worked in the People Department (that's Southwest speak for HR) at Southwest Airlines for 10 years and has great insight into the Southwest hiring process. In fact, she helped develop it. Career Takeoff also provides LOI preparation as part of their service. However, Career Takeoff is not limited to just SWA, they provide interview preparation for all airlines. I encourage you to research these companies and decide for yourself; it's an investment in your future!

Both Emerald Coast and FAPA are great resources for recent trip reports. Another great resource for trip reports is The Pilot Network (TPN) website www.thepilotnetwork.org. Trip reports are post-interview summaries of the interview experience from pilots who have recently interviewed at XYZ airlines. In terms you are more familiar with as a military pilot, a trip report is "the gouge" on what you can expect when you interview there. Trip reports are a great source of current intelligence covering everything from travel logistics (recommended hotels, transportation to the interview, etc.) to specific questions asked in the interview. The "bro network" is also a great source for getting your hands on recent trip reports. If you know someone who has interviewed recently, ask him or her for a trip report.

Simply attending an interview-preparation seminar alone will not make you an expert at interviewing. You will need to practice the skills you learn in seminar over and over again until they are second nature! You should use trip reports to start practicing your responses to potential interview questions at home. A technique I found very useful (and free) was to participate in informal study groups with my peers who were also preparing for airline interviews. Grab a stack of trip reports and start firing questions at each other over beer and pizza. You will be able to garner some great techniques by listening to the way your peers respond to various types of questions. The more you practice, the more polished and natural your responses will be, and your confidence will grow with each session.

In addition to polishing your interview skills, you should do your homework on the airline you're applying to. Research the company's history, their core values, their fleet, and their domiciles. Have they won any recent industry awards? Do they have any business initiatives ongoing? This should sound vaguely familiar since most of it is the same information I recommended you research for attending a job fair. Most of this information can be found on the airline's website, but there are also books that have been written about most of the major airlines. Airline-specific books are a great way to understand an airline's history and culture.

I'll be honest here; I applied to almost as many airlines as I have fingers (for the record, I have all my digits), but I did not read a book for every airline I applied to. I would recommend reading up on your top three targeted airlines as a minimum. Here is a not-so-all-inclusive list of books you may want to consider reading while researching some of the major airlines you may be targeting:

AIRLINE	BOOK TITLE
Delta Air Lines	*Delta: The History of an Airline* By W. David Lewis & Wesley Phillips Newton
Delta Air Lines	*Glory Lost and Found* By Seth Kaplan and Jay Shabat
United Airlines	*The Age of Flight: A History of America's Pioneering Airline* By William Garvey
American Airlines	*American Airlines, US Airways and the Creation of the World's Largest Airline* By Ted Reed
American Airlines	*Silverbird* By Don Bedwell and John Wegg
Southwest Airlines	*Nuts!* By Kevin and Jackie Freiberg
Southwest Airlines	*Lead with LUV: A Different Way to Create Real Success* By Ken Blanchard and Colleen Barrett
Federal Express	*The World On Time* By James C. Wetherbe
Federal Express	*Changing How the World Does Business* By Roger Frock
UPS	*Big Brown* By Greg Niemann
JetBlue Airways	*Blue Streak* By Barbara Peterson

Table 3. Airline History Recommended Reading List

If you have a really short-notice interview and just don't have the time to read an entire book, there is a pretty good book that gives a brief summary of the history of several of the major airlines. It's called *Airlines of the United States Since 1914*, by R. E. G. Davies. It will at least give you the salient high points of the legacy air carriers.

Aviation General-Knowledge Test

What? Nobody told me there would be a test! Well, now you can't say that, because I just told you. Some airlines do make you take a written general-knowledge test as part of your interview process. Delta and FedEx are two major airlines that use knowledge tests. Obviously, the sooner you start studying the better; you don't want to wait until you get called for an interview. So it's time to dust off those old textbooks and start studying like your job depended on it, because it just might. **Remember, getting a job is a full-time job!**

Trip reports will often have some of the questions included on the test, but be careful using "gouge" as your only study source. It's very probable that the test questions are randomly generated from a large master question bank, so there's no guarantee the questions on the trip report will be the same questions you get on your test. Also, you are relying on someone's memory to accurately recall the test questions after his or her interview. Having been through a few interviews myself, I can tell you that your brain is usually scrambled eggs after the interview. Often, you will see trip reports that list the question and what the author of the trip report thinks is the correct answer. Use extreme caution in relying on test-question answers found in trip reports...you would be wise to look up the answer on your own.

The best way to prepare for an aviation-knowledge test is to study and gain a solid foundation of the subject matter rather than try to memorize individual questions and answers. Delta Air Lines sends their interview candidates a very comprehensive list of subjects to study that fall into four major categories: aerodynamics, aircraft systems, air navigation, and aviation meteorology. Because you have made it this far into the book and you're still reading it, I have included a copy of the Delta study guide with the Free Resources zip file available for download at www.cockpit2cockpit.com/shop

The Delta study guide includes a list of reference books that are great for brushing up on your aviation general knowledge, but there is one book that's not on their list that I consider a "must have." It's called *Everything Explained for the Professional Pilot*, by Richie Lengel. This book is an essential for any pilot's library regardless of whether you need to take a knowledge test or not. I constantly find myself referring to this book for answers to aviation-related questions. If you are using it to study for a test, I recommend looking up individual subjects in the index rather than reading the book cover to cover. This will save you a lot of wasted time, because the aviation-knowledge tests given in airline interviews don't cover some topics, such as Federal Aviation Regulations (FARs). There are several "pilot math" problems included on the test (60:1 rule, descent planning, etc.). The book *Everything Explained for the Professional Pilot* has an excellent "Rule of Thumb" section in the back that has some easy methods for solving pilot math problems. Another excellent resource is the FAA *Pilot's Handbook of Aeronautical Knowledge*.

If you really want to make sure you know your stuff for the aviation general-knowledge test, there is also a pay-for-membership website you can use to help prepare for the test. The company is Ready, Set, Takeoff (RST), and the website is www.readysettakeoff.com.

RST offers online training and interview preparation for a one-time fee of $299. Better yet, they guarantee you will pass the test or your money back. RST no longer requires that you have an airline interview scheduled before you sign up for their services. They have created the RST Preview platform to allow anybody to get a head-start with the interview preparation process. The cost of the RST Preview package is $399.

In addition to aviation general knowledge test preparation, your fee also covers access to recent trip reports, cognitive-skills test practice, HR panel interview preparation, videos, flash-card trainers and other resources. They also offer personality test preparation. Disclaimer: I have not personally used RST, however, I have read many positive reviews about this amazing service.

Cognitive-Skills Test

Some airlines use cognitive-skills tests during the interview process. These tests are designed to measure your eye-hand coordination, ability to multitask, and ability to quickly scan, interpret, process, and react to information. Essentially, they want to make sure your noggin functions in a way that is compatible with the skills required of a pilot. The cognitive-skills test is actually a series of mini tests, each designed to test a different part of the brain such as information processing, memory, attention, visual construction, visual learning, and spatial analyses. Airlines that use cognitive-skills tests in the interview process include American, Delta, and FedEx.

Research findings have demonstrated that information-processing ability (i.e., attention, selection, internalization, and use of information) is crucial in determining how pilots make effective decisions during complex aviation situations.[6] Expert decision-making needed for successful pilot performance also necessitates elevated memory capacity, perceptual superiority, problem analysis, and performance speed and accuracy. In other words, these tests will validate that you are the superhuman that you already think you are.

This portion of the interview can last anywhere from one hour to several hours depending on the airline. I am convinced that part of the test is just monitoring your reactions while you take the test to see if you get stressed or frustrated with the mind-numbing, seemingly never-ending series of trivial tasks or if you stay cool as a cucumber with a smile on your face that says, "Is that all? What else ya got?" So how are you supposed to prepare for that?

I know plenty of airline pilots who didn't prepare at all for this portion of the interview and did just fine. That's a bit risky in my opinion, given what's on the line. At a minimum, I recommend researching each section of the cognitive-skills test that is used by the airline you are interviewing with by reading previous trip reports. At least understand what the test consists of and the basic instructions for each subtest. Knowing what to expect will increase your confidence and help you relax.

Some of the more common cognitive-skills subtests include substituting symbols for digits, completing a visual matrix by selecting from multiple-choice options, identifying missing aspects or items within picture representations, and tests that asses the ability to visualize complete objects from disassembled parts and to mentally construct two-dimensional representations of abstract objects. Tests assessing working memory often involve the immediate and delayed recall of sequential strings of digits, recalling them both forward and backward, as well as memorizing word lists and the visual display of items. Processing-speed tests often include visual-discrimination tasks and coding tasks requiring vertical and horizontal tracking, and they can entail reproducing or selecting a corresponding symbol to the presented target stimulus item.

As you have already seen, the *Cockpit to Cockpit* website is full of resources to help you succeed in your journey from military to airline pilot. Included in the

---

6 M. J. Bates, C. D. Colwell, R. E. King, F. M. Siem, and W. E. Zelenski, *Pilot Performance Variables (AL/CF-TR-1997-0059)* (Wright-Patterson AFB, OH: Crew Systems Directorate Human Engineering Division, 1997).

Free Resources zip file (available for download from the "Shop" link) are several PowerPoint practice tests, including some of the cognitive-skills tests used by American, Delta, and FedEx. Additionally, there are descriptions of various cognitive-skills tests used by several airlines.

If you want to go one step further to make sure you are fully prepared, there are a few brain-training websites you can use to practice cognitive skills. The practice tests used on these websites won't be the exact same tests you will face in the interview, but they do help train your brain in performing the same functions that the airlines are testing. I used a site called www.lumosity.com. Lumosity allows you to use some of their website for free, or you can pay a nominal monthly fee for full access. Another similar website is www.happy-neuron.com.

Line-Oriented Interview (LOI)

So you have aced the general-knowledge test, impressed the HR folks with your charming personality in the panel interview, and scored off the charts in the cognitive-skills tests...what else can they throw at you? How about a timed role-play scenario in which you are the captain and you have to handle an in-flight emergency (IFE) that requires a divert to the nearest suitable airfield? The LOI is designed to evaluate your ability to handle stress, your CRM skills, and your decision-making methodology.

Southwest Airlines uses the LOI as part of their interview process. They will put you in a room with a paper tiger (a cockpit mock-up with posters of the various cockpit panels). Don't worry; you don't need to know anything about the cockpit setup, switches, radios, and so on. The paper tiger is just there to add realism to the scenario and make you feel like you're in an airline cockpit. Two interviewers will act as your first officer and another pilot jump seater. They will also play the role of anyone else you need to talk to during the scenario, including flight attendants, ATC, dispatch, and MedLink.

The interviewers will very clearly brief the rules of engagement (ROE) for the scenario before they start the clock, a countdown timer displayed on your instrument panel. Once the scenario begins, you will have seven minutes to handle the IFE, divert, and land. Seven minutes sounds like a long time, but when you are busy handling all the distractions they will throw at you during the scenario, it seems like thirty seconds!

After the clock reaches zero, the interviewers will leave the room for about five minutes to allow you to collect your thoughts. When they return to the room, they will ask you to debrief them on how the scenario went. There is a dry-erase board with markers in the room that you can use for the debriefing if you wish. I just treated this like a condensed military sortie debriefing (you know us fighter guys; given the chance, we'll debrief ourselves to death). Talk about what went right, what went wrong, and what else you would have liked to do if you had another minute on the clock. Hint: when you debrief, make sure you discuss what "we" did right and wrong, not just what "I" did right and wrong. Remember, this is a CRM evaluation, and you are not the only crewmember.

The FedEx interview process includes an LOI that is almost identical to the Southwest LOI. It is also a timed scenario, but FedEx gives you eight minutes to work the problem (as you know, Southwest likes to do everything faster). Instead of a paper tiger, FedEx uses a desktop trainer that you "fly" during the scenario, but the emphasis is on your CRM skills, not your computer flying skills.

The two best ways to prepare for the LOI are taking an interview-preparation course that specializes in LOI interviews and practicing with other friends who are also applying to the airlines. As part of the Emerald Coast class, Aaron "Albie" Hagan does an excellent job of providing a simple formula for handling any scenario. As a former member of the Southwest Airlines pilot hiring team, Rebekah Krone also provides specialized LOI training as part of the Career Takeoff interview preparation services.

Once you and your other military friends have attended an LOI preparation class, get together and practice various scenarios with each other. Use a countdown timer to add that extra element of stress. The more you practice, the more confidence you will build in being able to handle any scenario they throw at you within the allotted time limit.

United Airlines has a line-oriented portion of their interview with a slightly different twist. Instead of a timed scenario, United uses more of a technical-skills interview followed by a CRM discussion. United will send a study packet to their interview candidates ahead of time to familiarize candidates with United callouts and procedures as well as to familiarize candidates with the Electronic Flight Bag (EFB). The EFB is a tablet computer containing all the approach plates, Standard Instrument Departures (SIDS), Standard Terminal Arrivals (STARS), flight manuals, checklists, and so on.

During the technical-skills interview, the interviewer will brief the ROE before the scenario begins. You will be given one of four scenarios, such as a flight from Las Vegas to John F. Kennedy International. You will be provided the flight route along with weather and NOTAMS. The interviewer will then ask you a series of technical questions about SIDS, STARS, instrument approaches, and so on, in a logical sequence, as he or she steps you through each phase of the flight. You may be asked about United callouts from the study material that was sent to you. You will probably be expected to give a departure brief and an arrival brief, to include briefing the Jeppesen approach plate. At some point, the interviewer will give you an IFE to handle and expect you to run the appropriate checklist from the EFB. There will also be a divert scenario at some point to evaluate your decision-making and CRM skills.

Your best bet to prepare for the United technical-skills interview is to get your hands on the gouge (trip reports and talking to your friends who have already interviewed). Most trip reports will give the scenario and questions they got asked. The *Everything Explained for the Professional Pilot* book by Richie Lengel is also an excellent study source that even gives examples of how to do a departure brief and how to brief an instrument-approach plate.

Once the technical-skills portion of the interview is complete, United then does a CRM discussion in which they will show you a quick video of a flight scenario in which CRM played a factor. After the video you will be asked to debrief the CRM skills (or lack thereof) in the video and what you would do differently. This portion should be a no-brainer. As a military pilot you have been exposed to CRM training of the highest caliber. Just do some of that pilot shit, Mav!

Simulator Evaluation

Several years ago, there were a few airlines that used a simulator evaluation as part of their interview process, including FedEx, United, and UPS. A simulator evaluation is exactly what it sounds like. They put you in an airline simulator and evaluate your flying skills. Most airlines that used to include this in their interview process have dropped it due to the high cost of operating the simulators (roughly twenty to thirty dollars per minute!) and the limited scheduling availability of simulators. All except UPS, that is.

If you interview at UPS, you will get a chance to fly their MD-11 simulator. UPS is the only major airline that still includes a simulator evaluation as part of their interview.

I have heard from some UPS pilots that it's not necessary to pay for simulator instruction to prepare for a UPS interview. Most candidates do just fine without it. Maybe for those who have never flown a heavy aircraft before and have their heart set on flying for UPS, that might be a consideration, but honestly I don't think you need to spend the $1000 to $1500. It sounds like the UPS simulator evaluation is more of a formality than anything (see details in the next paragraph). If your heart is still set on doing some simulator-interview preparation, there is a company that offers MD-11 simulator instruction to prepare candidates for the UPS interview. The company is Adam Hughes Consulting (www.adamhughes.vpweb.com/default.html).

The UPS simulator evaluation is very straightforward. You will receive a very thorough briefing on what you are looking at, the basics of flying the aircraft, and the profile including basic instructions on how to fly each maneuver. The simulator will be hand-flown (no autopilot) without visuals or motion. Only the instruments and avionics will be active. The "evaluation" is actually very instructional, and you can expect a lot of coaching throughout the profile. The profile consists of a normal takeoff, level off, steep turns, vectors to an ILS, and a go-around.

Personality-Screening Tests

Would you believe me if I told you that you could serve honorably as a very successful career military officer, pass all the rigorous tests and interviews listed above, and still be rejected by an airline because of a personality-screening test? I wouldn't have believed it either until it happened to me.

The Delta Air Lines interview is a two-day process. The first day consists of a panel interview, a ball-buster aviation-knowledge test (forgive the term, ladies, but any guy who has been kicked in the junk knows what I'm talking about here), a grueling series of cognitive-skills tests, and a short personality-screening test (about fifty true/false questions). If you do well on day one, Delta offers you a conditional job offer (CJO) and invites you back for day two of the interview.

On the second day, Delta has you take a more in-depth personality test called the Minnesota Multiphasic Personality Inventory (MMPI-2). It's a more expanded version of the personality test taken on day one, but this one consists of 567 true/false questions. The MMPI-2 is designed to detect maladjustment or clinically diagnosed psychiatric conditions that your typical serial killer or pedophile might be afflicted with. After taking the MMPI-2 test, you interview with a psychologist. Unlike that of other airlines, the Delta day-one panel interview is more situation-based questions to see how you would handle various scenarios. The day-two psychologist interview is where you will be asked the TMAAT questions that you practiced with your interview-preparation service (Emerald Coast, FAPA, etc.). However, they won't be asked in the same direct manner you practiced. For example, instead of asking you, "Tell me about a time you were stressed," the psychologist may ask you, "What was the most stressful time in your life?" They are still asking the same question, but they are asking it in a supersneaky head-shrink way. Don't let it throw you off. Anyway, if Delta detects any irregularities based on your day-two psychological screening, they will e-mail you to inform you that your records are being referred to a legal board called the Pilot Application Review Board (PARB).

The PARB process can take anywhere from one to six weeks. You do not get the opportunity to meet or speak with the PARB. Your records, including your interview and personality-testing results, application, military performance evaluations, and résumé go before the board. The PARB consists of a chief pilot, a representative from the Delta Air Lines legal department, a representative from HR, and the contract psychologist who interviewed you. According to Delta Air Lines chief pilot for pilot hiring, legal has the final decision authority on the PARB. He also stated that in most cases the PARB recommends to hire the pilot applicant. Unfortunately, if the PARB decides not to hire you, then you will receive a "thanks for playing" call from the Delta chief pilot for pilot hiring (a nice personal touch), and you will be told that you may never apply to Delta Air Lines again…game over.

Delta was the first interview invite I received after retiring from the air force. I had a stellar air-force career as demonstrated by a ROP full of officer evaluations that highlighted superior performance, achievement, strong work ethic, and high moral character as well as multiple Commendation, Air and Aerial Achievement, and Meritorious Service Medals. Despite all that and being offered a CJO after passing the day-one tests and interviews, I was ultimately rejected by Delta based on the results of my personality screening.

The only feedback I received was that I tested "unusually positive" to the point of being outside the range of a normal person on the MMPI-2. They offered me a chance to retake the test before meeting with the psychologist with the advice to "not be so positive this time." I retook the test and tried to change a few answers to be less positive. The results of my second test were never disclosed to me other than to say that they were "valid" as opposed to my first "invalid" attempt.

I recall sitting in the waiting area after the second test attempt feeling quite rattled. Everything up to this point had gone great, but after taking a 567-question true/false psychological-screening test twice, I must admit my brain was fried. The interview with the psychologist did not go well at all. The lesson here for you is, stick to your game plan. Your interview-preparation service will give you a standard format for responding to TMAAT questions. Even if you have to retake the MMPI-2, you will probably be OK as long as you stick to your game plan.

In the wake of the Germanwings Flight 9525 incident in 2015 in which a pilot committed suicide by intentionally crashing an A-320 into the mountains, killing 144 passengers and 6 crewmembers in the process, I can understand why personality-screening tests are necessary. Unfortunately, I think some very good people (myself included) get screened out due to a certain small percentage of false positives on these tests.

American, United, and UPS use similar personality-screening tests during their pre-interview application process. We already discussed the American Airlines Organizational Fit Assessment in chapter 6. The OFA is part of the American Airlines application process on pilotcredentials.com.

If United Airlines or UPS is considering you for an interview, they will send you an electronic link to take the Hogan Personality Inventory (HPI) online. The HPI consists of 206 true/false questions. Unlike the MMPI-2, which is focused on discovering various forms of psychopathology, the HPI is more focused on measuring positive and negative personality traits for pilots. If you pass the HPI, United will then send you an interview invitation. If you don't pass, they will send you a "no, thank you" e-mail stating that you may apply again one year from the date of the e-mail. According to the senior manager of pilot hiring at United Airlines, many of their pilots fail the HPI the first time only to pass it a year later and get hired at United Airlines.

There are a few paid website services out there that claim they can train you to "pass" these personality tests. I'm not advocating that you should game the system or answer the test questions dishonestly. However, I don't think there is anything wrong with educating yourself about these personality tests so you have a better understanding of the type of questions you will be asked and to lower your apprehension level so you will test with a clear mind and lessen the chances of being screened out due to false positives.

My motivation for writing *Cockpit to Cockpit* is to provide future military pilots seeking airline careers with the "transition gouge." I want you to have access to the lessons learned from those who have gone through the transition process before you to increase your chances of getting hired by your airline of choice. Therefore, I have done some research for you regarding airline personality-screening tests.

Certain personality traits may be considered relatively healthy in day-to-day functions but may be maladaptive and elevate the risk for adjustment difficulties, performance problems, and adaption to various physically or psychologically high-risk, high-demand conditions and occupational-duty positions (such as flying a multimillion dollar jet and being responsible for the lives of hundreds of passengers).

Again, the MMPI-2 is designed to detect maladjustment or clinically diagnosed psychiatric conditions. Each clinical condition is given a scale on which the test participant's responses are scored. What is important to know about the MMPI-2 is that the assessment contains validity scales that can raise red flags and lead to "invalid" test results based on the response patterns to select questions. The specific validity scale that is most sensitive in the job-selection context is one that assesses response inflation—a manifestation of positive impression management, what is commonly known to the psych docs as "faking good."

Obviously, you want to put your best foot forward in the interview process and make a positive impression. Those who produce an invalid profile on this scale when completing the test are not typically responding in a fashion driven by ill-motivated faking; however, when this validity scale is elevated, it is commonly interpreted as not responding to questions in an honest or forthcoming fashion. One piece of advice that I received from a psychologist involved in assessment and selection programs is: "Be wary of dichotomous, all-or-none-type language such as 'always' or 'never.' If a test taker does not admit to the most minor of character flaws, their profile will be interpreted as invalid, and it will be assumed that they approached the test in a defensive manner."

As you are answering the true/false questions on the personality-screening test, answer honestly, but if you find a few that you're not quite sure which way to answer, then ask yourself this: is this question asking about a minor character flaw that is common to most people (i.e., an "acceptable" character flaw), or is this a red-flag character flaw that would indicate an abnormality? That should guide your response.

If you would like to read more on this subject, I have provided a brief summary of industry-standard personality tests included in the Free Resources zip file available for download on the *Cockpit to Cockpit* website "Shop" link with an in depth discussion of the various personality traits and scales being measured by these tests along with characteristics considered desirable and undesirable for pilots.

Logbook Interview

Although all the airlines will look at your logbooks, only Southwest Airlines conducts a separate logbook interview. The other airlines will review your logbooks and flight records in private while you are busy with the other portions of the interview. The SWA logbook interview seems to serve three purposes:

1. Verify your application flight times, ratings, and certificates are accurate
2. Another chance to get to know the real you through informal conversation
3. Another chance for them to see how you react to stressful situations

I'm basing these assumptions on personal experience and from feedback gathered from multiple trip reports and TPN posts.

As a military pilot, the logbook interview should be the lowest threat portion of the SWA interview process as long as you have done a good job preparing your logbooks, assuming you have any besides your military flight records that should speak for themselves. During my logbook interview we spent less than ten minutes looking at my logbooks, and the rest of the time having fun, casual conversation (but don't get too relaxed, it's still an interview).

I have heard of some pilots getting the "bad cop" treatment in the logbook interview to see how you react to stress. You may get questioned on how you derived a certain flight time total like PIC, or cross-country time, etc. You may even be told you didn't do it correctly. No need to panic and **definitely don't get defensive with the interviewer.** If you get this kind of treatment they are really just trying to see how well you handle stress. Apologize for the error, and offer to correct the problem on the spot. Test done, you passed.

Another method they might use to see how you handle stress is to ask for something that was not included in the pre-interview instructions. For instance, they might hand you a calculator and ask for your flight time totals for each year going back five years. Since I had read that in several trip reports, I already had a spreadsheet prepared with the requested information. I just handed it to the interviewer and he was happy with that.

Airline-Specific Interview Formats

Here is a brief summary of the interview format for some of the more popular airlines you may be targeting. This information was gathered either from personal experience or from someone who has recently interviewed at the airline in question. These formats have been known to change from time to time. If you find that any of the info in table 4 below is not current, please use the "Contact Us" link on www.cockpit2cockpit.com to let us know.

AIRLINE	PRE-INTERVIEW	DAY 1	DAY 2
American Airlines	Organizational Fit Assessment Video Interview	Cognitive Skills Test	HR Panel Interview
Delta Air Lines	NA	Aviation Knowledge Test Cognitive Skill Test Personality Test HR Panel Interview	Drug Test (pee in a cup) MMPI-2 Personality Test Psychologist Interview
FedEx	NA	Aviation Knowledge Test Cognitive Skill Test Personality Test	HR Panel Interview LOI
JetBlue Airways	Video Interview	HR Panel Interview Cognitive Skill Test Personality Test	NA
Southwest Airlines		HR Panel Interview LOI Logbook Interview	NA
United Airlines	Hogan Personality Test	HR Panel Interview LOI (CRM & Technical)	NA
UPS		HR Panel Interview Simulator Evaluation	NA

Table 4. Airline Interview Formats

If the airline you are targeting is not listed in table 4, other good resources to get specific information about interview formats at your targeted airlines include the company website "Career" or "Work Here" links, trip reports from Emerald Coast, FAPA, or TPN, the Airline Pilot Central forums, and the good old "bro" network.

Summary

Well, that's it; you've done everything you can do to prepare for the interview. You worked with an interview-preparation service, read up on the airlines you're targeting, practiced interview skills with friends and family, brushed up on your aviation general knowledge, practiced some cognitive-skills tests online, and learned about the various personality-screening tests. You are ready!

In the next chapter, we will discuss the actual interview. I will give you some packing tips and discuss how to conduct yourself during and after the interview to increase your odds of getting the job.

THE CHECKLIST

- **Consider signing up for an interview-preparation service.**
- **Obtain copies of recent airline interview trip reports.**
- **Practice interview questions with friends, family, or coworkers until the responses are natural.**
- **Research the airlines you are targeting.**
- **Read any applicable books written about your top three targeted airlines.**
- **Start studying for the aviation general-knowledge test. Consider using Ready, Set, Takeoff (FedEx and Delta).**
- **Consider using an online cognitive-skills training website to practice for cognitive-skills tests.**
- **Consider an LOI preparation class. Practice line-oriented interview techniques (Southwest and FedEx) with friends.**
- **Study trip reports to learn about the line-oriented interview (United). Practice with friends.**
- **Research the MMPI-2 and Hogan personality screening tests. Consider using a personality screening practice test service.**
- **Consider taking a simulator interview-preparation course if you have never flown a heavy aircraft (UPS).**

CHAPTER 9

The Interview and Beyond

Interview Logistics

ALL YOUR HARD work up to this point should result in an interview invite. You will either get a call or an e-mail from the airline with instructions for scheduling an interview, making nonrevenue (free) travel arrangements on their airline, what to bring, and so on. You want to take the earliest interview date and time available, because it will ultimately translate to a higher seniority number when you get hired. Delaying an interview by even a few days can bump you into a later class date. The difference of just a few seniority numbers higher can mean the difference between getting the aircraft or domicile assignment you want and not getting it.

Here are a few tips on packing for the big day. If you are flying to the interview, do your best to carry on everything you need and avoid any checked bags. Checked bags sometimes get lost, and you can't afford to have that happen to anything you need for the interview. If you absolutely must check a bag, try to put your nonessentials in the checked bag. Ideally you should have everything needed for your interview, including clothes and paperwork, in your carry-on. That is easier said than done, especially if it's a two-day interview.

One of the hardest things to do is organize and hand-carry the mountain of paperwork they will ask you to bring. I recommend making tab-divided binders with a table of contents up front so everything looks organized and professional. This is more for you to stay organized than it is for them. The airline will likely deconstruct your binders, take out what they need, and hand you back the binder and tab dividers. They will ask for a copy of your military flight records and any logbooks you have if you have kept your own logbooks (see chapter 3). Make sure you bring a copy of your entire military flight records, not just the two-to-three-page summary documents. Also, do not give them any original copies of required paperwork unless they insist on it.

For carrying all the paperwork, you will want a professional-looking briefcase or shoulder-bag portfolio case. Don't be the guy or gal who shows up in a nice interview suit and a backpack...seriously? You're not twelve! Also, a rolling portfolio bag looks a little dorky in an interview, but that's just my opinion.

Be a Team Player

Depending on the airline, there could be as few as six or as many as twenty-five other pilot candidates interviewing in your allocated date/time slot. When you show up on the day of your interview, you will meet the other candidates in your group. Keep in mind that they *are not* the competition. The airline wants to hire every candidate they interview. The HR personnel will be watching, even during the "dead time" between interview activities, to see how you interact with your fellow candidates, administrative staff, and even janitorial workers. You want to be seen as the team player. Here are a few things you can do to be the hero of the group.

It's generally a long day of activities with very few breaks. Bring some granola bars or snack-size bags of trail mix in your bag to share with your group. Also bring an emergency kit with mouthwash, floss, lint brush, shoe shine pad, and so on. Ask if anybody needs these items. Bring an extra tie in case you or one of your fellow interviewees nukes themselves with ketchup during the lunch break. Tip: don't eat anything that involves sauce or grease for breakfast or lunch!

Bring a legal pad and pen. At the first opportunity, start a contact roster to get your fellow candidate's names, phone numbers, and e-mails. The purpose of the contact roster is to keep each other informed after the interview. The time between the interview and actually getting the job offer can be nerve-racking, especially if there is no news. Keep each other informed so you will all know where you stand in the process. A simple e-mail to the group to say, "Hey, my references are getting calls" or "I received a request from the airline for additional information" can really help everyone gauge where they stand in the process. You will definitely want to know when others in the group get the job offer or "no thanks" call. It's also a nice gesture to provide support to those who get rejected by offering to stay in touch and help them in the future. You would want someone to do the same for you.

A "Thank You" Goes a Long Way

As you go through your interview process, try to collect business cards of the key players you interact with from the airline HR department, including administrative personnel, interviewers, and anyone else who played a role in organizing and conducting the logistics of the day. If they don't have a business card, at least write down their name (make sure you get the correct spelling). You also want to get the mailing address for the pilot-hiring department. The reason you're gathering these names is that you're going to send thank-you notes after the interview. Right now you're probably saying to yourself, "No way, I'm not gonna do that"...Yes, you are!

We talked about it multiple times throughout this book; the airlines have plenty of qualified applicants. They are looking for the pilot willing to go the extra mile. Thank-you notes are part of the extra mile. They can also partially make up for an interview question or two that maybe didn't go as well as you would have liked. Worse yet, you may not even know that you bombed a response to one of their questions, but the interviewers picked up on something in one of your responses that came off as a little arrogant or prickly (that's prick with an "ly" added to it). The personal thank-you note can help them look past a few interview hiccups. You can also use it to help subtly address any known interview hiccups while thanking them for their time.

You can write one note to the entire interview and HR team, or you can really knock their socks off by writing individual notes to each team member. If you take the former approach, at least try to address each team member by name somewhere in the thank-you note. There is a good sample thank-you note you can use as a guide included with the *Cockpit to Cockpit* support package products.

Write a Trip Report

Remember all those great trip reports you read that helped you prepare for your interview? Well, it's time to pay it forward. You owe it to the next group of interviewees to help them get the latest gouge on what the interview process is like at XYZ airlines. If you have some dead time between interview activities, use the time to write down as many questions and details as you can remember from the HR panel interview, aviation knowledge test, LOI scenario, and so on. Especially, take note of anything that caught you off guard.

Although there is no set format for a trip report, there are a few key elements that should be included. One of those key elements is to disclose if you got hired or rejected. Some airlines like Delta will tell you right away. Other airlines like JetBlue, Southwest, and American make you wait anywhere between two and six weeks. If you don't know right away, you can always go back and update your trip report later, but don't delay writing the trip report while waiting for words back from the airline, because if you're anything like me, the longer you wait the more information you will forget.

If you got rejected, there is no shame in saying so on a trip report. Help out the next applicants by letting them know where you think you may have screwed up. Most trip reports are written anonymously anyway.

You will want to include your background and the background of your interview group on the trip report, along with who got hired and who didn't (and why they didn't get hired if you know it). Here is an example:

> *My stats: F-16, T-37, T-6 IP, 3500 hrs total time*
> *8 interviewed in my group: 5 military (3 heavy, 2 fighter), 3 civilian (2 regional airlines, 1 corporate aviation). 7 male, 1 female.*
> *6/8 hired (5 male, 1 female). The corporate pilot and one of the heavy pilots not hired. The corporate pilot said he thought he bombed the knowledge test. The heavy pilot said he didn't think he did well on the situational-based questions in the HR interview.*

If you recall the beginning of your airline-application journey, you probably remember wondering what kind of timeline to expect from submitting the application to actually getting hired and starting training. It would be nice of you to include that information on your trip report to help out those behind you. Your trip report should include approximate dates for the following milestones:

a. Date application submitted
b. Date received interview invite
c. Date of interview
d. Date of hired notification
e. Date of initial training class

It's also nice to provide some gouge on logistics of getting to the interview. Did the airline provide complimentary positive-space round-trip air travel (most airlines do) to the interview? Where is the best place to stay? Does the hotel offer an airline discount rate for interviews (many do, but you have to ask)? Did you need to rent a car, or does the hotel provide shuttle service to and from the airport and interview location (usually company headquarters)? These are all questions you should provide answers to in the logistics portion of your trip report.

Of course, the main reason to write a trip report is to give future pilot candidates the most detailed information possible about the actual interview. Try to take notes throughout the day during your interview process on anything you can recall that would be useful to include in your trip report. Your trip report should include an overview of the interview format and as many specific test and interview questions as you can recall, along with any other information you think might be useful to future interview candidates. There is a good trip report template available to you as part of the *Cockpit to Cockpit* support package products available at www.cockpit-2cockpit.com.

Once you're done writing your trip report, you need to find a way to get it out there to the masses. One of the best ways to do that is to send a copy to the interview-preparation service you used so they can share it with their clients. You probably got many of the trip reports you used to prepare for your interview the same way. It's also a way to provide feedback to the interview-preparation service on how well (or, God forbid, how not well) they prepared you for the interview experience. Another great way to distribute your trip report is to send it to The Pilot Network so they can add it to their trip report collection on www.thepilotnetwork.org.

The Pilot Hiring Board

There are a few major airlines that will give you your interview results either the same day or within twenty-four hours. Delta Air Lines will either give you a conditional job offer (CJO) or a "thanks but no-thanks" (TBNT) at the end of the first day of their interview process. We were told upfront at the start of my Delta interview that Delta has a minimum passing score for each of the events involved in day-one of their interview process (see chapter 8, table 4). If you meet the minimum threshold score for each of the events, you will be offered a CJO and invited back for the day-two portion of the interview process (see chapter 8, table 4). If you get a TBNT after day one of the interview, you will be told you can reapply in six months. Most airlines have the same or similar policy. FedEx will call you that night, after you have finished the second day of the interview process, to either give you the TBNT or the CJO news.

Most major airlines use a pilot hiring board to make the final hiring decision. When the dust settles after the interview, the interview team will collect their notes about your interview performance along with their recommendation and forward it to the pilot hiring board. Generally speaking, a pilot hiring board will be convened every four to six weeks to make a final hiring decision on all the pilot interviews since the last hiring board.

The Southwest Airlines pilot hiring board consists of the pilot hiring manager, key HR personnel, and the chief pilot or assistant chief pilot from each domicile. I suspect other airlines use a similar composition for their pilot hiring board. You may think that other than the thank-you notes there is nothing else you can do after the interview to affect the chances of your getting hired...but you would be wrong about that.

Picture this; the pilot hiring board meets, either virtually, or in person. They have in front of them a file on each of the pilot candidates to be considered for that board. The leader of the team calls out the first pilot candidate's name being considered. "OK first up, is Holly Hulahan. Looks like most of her interview went fairly well, but she was a little weak on the LOI portion in terms of CRM and communicating the plan. Anyone have any additional information on her?" One of the domicile chief pilots responds, "Yeah, I had two of my pilots personally go to bat for Holly. They came to my office with hard-copy, signed recommendation letters and had nothing but positive praise for her flying skills and personality." Two other domicile chief pilots then tell similar stories. The board discusses and decides that they can overlook the slightly below average LOI performance based on the testimony of those who know Holly the best and have worked with her in the past.

Now contrast that scenario with candidate number two. The leader of the pilot hiring board continues, "All-right, next we have Bob Lipshits. Some of Bob's interview responses came off a little cocky, but he did OK on the other interview portions. Anyone have any additional information on Bob?" Crickets, crickets...nobody speaks up for Bob, therefore the pilot hiring board decides to give Bob a TBNT.

Hopefully these examples demonstrate how important it can be to have as many people as possible at the pilot hiring board show up prepared to go to bat for you. So how do you do that? First, make sure you ask during your interview when your pilot hiring board will happen. They may not give you an exact date, but they should be able to narrow it down to plus or minus a week. Next, call each of your internal recommendation references and tell them when you expect your pilot hiring board will take place. They probably want to hear how your interview experience went anyway. Ask them to hand-walk a hard copy of your recommendation letter to their domicile chief pilot and go to bat for you. If they can't get to the chief pilot in person, at least ask them to send an email with an electronic copy of the LOR to their domicile chief pilot. Ideally, you want to find someone you know at each domicile to go to their chief pilot on your behalf in order to maximize the number of chief pilots going to bat for you at the pilot hiring board. I realize that's probably unrealistic but do your best to cover as many domiciles as possible.

Getting the Call

The time between the airline interview and getting "the call" can be agonizing. Every time the phone rings and you see an unfamiliar number, your heart will skip a beat. Could this be it?

When you do get the call, it's a huge emotional release. You have worked very hard to fulfill this dream, and it's finally coming true. Congratulations! Try not to let your voice crack like a thirteen-year-old boy in puberty. There are a few key questions to ask before you hang up the phone to call your spouse, parents, and so on. Ask what the next step is in the process. Often there are more forms to fill out and more information needed by the airline. You will also want to ask when you will receive a training-class date. Sometimes that class date is many months in the future. If you are available sooner than that, make sure to tell them you are available on short notice in case any vacancies open up in earlier class dates (it happens more often than you would think). I know several pilots who were able to move their start date up as much as four months earlier because they spoke up on the initial call. That can translate to several hundred seniority numbers higher!

If you have really kicked ass and dedicated yourself to the "getting a job is a full-time job" concept, you may even get multiple job offers from two or more airlines. So if you're one of those lucky guys and gals who get hired by multiple airlines, what do you do when you get the second or third offer? Obviously you're going to take the first offer because you have nothing else in hand yet. If the first offer comes from your top choice of airlines, you might be tempted to politely turn down offers two and three. Whoa, whoa, whoa, Rambo...not so fast!

Nothing is certain until you have a class date! My business-savvy wife would take it one step further and say nothing is certain until the first paycheck clears the bank. My first airline offer came from JetBlue Airways. JetBlue called me in late December of 2014 to let me know that I had passed "Phase II" of the post-interview process, which meant I was officially in the pool awaiting a class-training date. Unfortunately, I didn't know that I was in the bottom of the deep end of the pool. JetBlue didn't offer me a training class until May 2015. I waited almost six months from interview to receiving an official job offer. If that sounds like a long time, I know friends who waited over a year with American and Delta.

There are several factors related to when you will start training with an airline, but the bottom line is that it's all about the needs of the airline, not your need for a job. It depends on how many were hired before you and how many they can put through training in a given time period. In the cases of JetBlue, American, and Delta mentioned above, they had hired many more pilots than their training pipeline could handle at the time. During that waiting period, you are not yet an airline employee. That means that if there is a sudden economic downturn, you could lose that job offer (hence the term "conditional" job offer).

So back to the original question: what do you do when you get the second or third offer? Say *yes!* Even if you think you won't end up at that airline, just say yes unless you already have a firm training date from your preferred airline and you are confident it won't be changed or taken away. You can always call them back later and change your mind, but it doesn't work the other way around (i.e., you can't say no initially and then call back later and say yes).

If you do say yes on the initial call, try to use some professionalism when you finally decide to burn that bridge and go with another offer. Professional courtesy dictates that you should give a company at least two weeks' notice (so they can try to fill the training slot you are vacating), but sometimes circumstances require you to not "show your cards" until the last minute. Don't feel too bad. How much notice do you think they are going to give you if they have to furlough you someday?

Summary

The way you treat others and interact with all airline employees and your fellow pilot candidates during the interview process can be just as important as the interview itself. Be kind, be courteous, and be a team player. Don't forget to take a few minutes between interview events to jot down some notes for the trip report you will write in the days after the interview to help the next pilot candidate succeed. Your fellow pilot candidates will consider you the group-hero if you take down their contact information and start the group e-mail to keep each other informed. Also, don't forget to get the HR department mailing address and the names of those you want to include in your thank-you notes.

After the interview, the waiting game begins, but in some cases your work is not done yet. If the airline uses a pilot hiring board, then you need to get as many pilots in as many domiciles as possible to go speak to their domicile chief pilot on your behalf before the hiring board. Have a plan for receiving job offers ahead of time, instead of waiting for the call to happen. Think about what you will do if you receive multiple offers. You might want to decide what your criteria will be for turning down a job offer. Don't assume just because you have a conditional job offer that you will be starting right away; have a plan for how you will handle being left in "the pool." Having a confirmed training start date is a huge security blanket!

In chapter 10 we will discuss my favorite topic in this book...paying it forward for the next military pilot. As you may recall, that was the main motivation for writing *Cockpit to Cockpit.*

THE CHECKLIST

- **Hand carry all items needed for the interview; only check bags as a last resort.**
- **Organize your paperwork in a professional-looking binder with labeled tab dividers and a table of contents.**
- **Create a contact roster with your fellow interview candidates to include name, e-mail, and phone numbers.**
- **Write down the names of all HR administrative staff and members of the pilot interview team and get an office address so you can send thank-you notes.**
- **During or immediately following the interview, jot down as many specific questions and details as possible to include in your trip report.**
- **Ask about the date of the pilot hiring board (if applicable).**
- **Try to get a pilot or employee at each airline domicile to speak to their domicile chief pilot on your behalf before the pilot hiring board (if applicable).**
- **Write a trip report within three days of your interview, while it's still fresh in your mind.**
- **Don't turn down any offers until you have a firm training date from the airline of your choice.**

CHAPTER 10

Congratulations, You're an Airline Pilot

Changing Teams

BEFORE I LAVISH you with well-deserved praise for your achievement, I need to sidebar one last time to discuss the decision to change airlines. Having made this leap of faith myself, I feel I would be doing you a disservice if I didn't provide you some wisdom regarding jumping ship from an airline.

Let me start by saying it's not a decision to be taken lightly. It's a significant emotional event when you move from one airline to another (not to mention a logistical pain in the ass). Make sure you discuss it with your family and have thought it through thoroughly.

Right now the airline industry is riding a historic high and is postured to remain that way for a long time. However, if history is any indicator, chances are the industry will suffer another setback sometime in the next twenty years. The measure of an airline's strength lies not in how well they perform in the good times, but in how well they weather the bad times.

There are several reasons why pilots change airlines. Location, pay, benefits, equipment and type of flying, and job security are probably the most common reasons. They are all valid reasons and there is no right or wrong answer. My advice to you is to ask yourself two questions. The first question is, "Which airline will provide me a better overall quality of life?" The second question is, "Which airline will still be standing when I am ready to retire?" If you're deciding between two very well established, financially-strong airlines, the second question may be a moot point.

If you're going to do it, the earlier the better. Obviously, the longer you wait, the more seniority you forfeit. When you start with another company, you start at the bottom of the seniority list. If you have been with your current airline for more than two years, is it worth starting over to you? It might be... it's a personal decision you will have to make.

If you think you might get a call from another airline and jump ship, you might want to research the 401K rules with your current company before you start investing with them. How long before your money is vested? With some airlines, you don't get to take 100 percent of your 401K with you to your new airline unless you have been there a certain amount of years. Therefore, you might consider holding off on investing in your 401K until you know you are going to stay, or until you start with your "forever airline."

Stay Cool When You're in the Pool

The excitement of receiving your first CJO from one of your top targeted airlines can be overwhelming. It's a very proud moment. You probably spent countless hours perfecting your résumé, cleaning up your logbooks, filling out applications, and preparing for the interview. You worked hard for this moment and now you want to share it with the world. The first thing most pilots do is change their Facebook profile picture to the tail flash of their new employer and blast out a social media message to their friends and family announcing the CJO. Here is just some food for thought on why you might want to hold off on making a social media announcement to the world.

You are now swimming in "the pool". In the aviation community, "the pool" is the term used to describe the time period between receiving the CJO and actually starting training. Recall our previous discussion from chapter 9 regarding airline training capacity and pool wait times. Some pilots only spend a few weeks in the pool, but others have been left in the deep end for up to a year without a flotation device.

One thing to keep in mind while you're treading water is that a Conditional Job Offer is just that...*Conditional.* You are not getting paid yet and although it is likely that the airline will get you into training at some point in the near future, it's not a guarantee. In September 2001, I was stationed at Sheppard AFB, Texas. The airlines were hiring again after a long layoff in the 1990s. I personally knew at least a dozen pilots who had recently been hired by the airlines. Some of them left the military at the twelve-to-eighteen-year point with no retirement. They bought nice houses in other cities where they were going to be domiciled with their new airline. Then somebody decided to crash a few airliners into the Pentagon and World Trade Center, and all of sudden those guys/gals were out on the street. The lucky ones had already started training and got furloughed. When you get furloughed, you keep your pilot seniority number with the understanding that at some undetermined point in the future, the airline will recall you to work. Until then you are essentially unemployed. It took over ten years for some of my pilot friends to be recalled to their airlines after being furloughed in the days after 9/11. The unlucky ones were waiting in the pool, and had their CJO's taken away.

Even if the situation is not as extreme as the one I just mentioned, you need to consider the possibility that even if this CJO is from your top choice airline, depending on how long they leave you in the pool, you might need to take interviews with other airlines just to put food on the table. Of course that depends on your personal financial situation.

The other possibility is that the first CJO you receive *is not* from your top choice airline and you were already planning to take interview invites from airlines that were rank ordered higher up your "dream sheet" list.

My point is that you really need to consider how smart it is to blow up your social media profile with your CJO and the logo of the airline that just hired you? The next airline you interview with just might (read: probably will) do a Google search on you and it would be awkward to say the least if you are interviewing at Delta and your Facebook profile picture is the American Airlines tail flash!

Consider this CJO like your first combat deployment. You wanted to tell your friends and family where you were going and when you would be back, but Operational Security (OPSEC) required you to stay silent. You probably want to make sure your spouse resists the temptation to announce your CJO on his/her social media accounts also, just in case.

OK, it's not quite as serious as OPSEC. I'm not saying you can't call your friends and family to announce your recent success; phone calls don't leave a trail of breadcrumbs for potential employers to follow. I'm just cautioning you against using social media as your messaging platform because social media is very easy for most anyone to see. Type in any name into the Facebook search bar (a name that is not already one of your contacts) and you will see what I'm talking about. You can see profile pictures at a minimum, and sometimes you can get a lot more information than that depending on the security settings that person has established on their social media account. However, even if you think you have your accounts locked down so nobody except those you have given permissions to can see your information, I still wouldn't risk it.

So when is it safe to make your big announcement to the world on social media? After all, you worked really hard to get to this point in life and there is nothing wrong with basking in the moment if the conditions are correct. I would offer you two conditions to meet before you make a social media CJO announcement:

1. The airline has given you a confirmed class start date. Once you have a class start date, chances are pretty good that this is for real. If you want to play more conservative you could wait until you actually start class and have a company ID badge (which usually happens on the first day of training).
2. You are 100% certain that this is the airline you want to retire from at age 65. If this airline was not your #1 choice, or at least an airline that you are happy to call your new #1, then hold off on any social media announcements. As mentioned previously, you don't want to be in the situation of interviewing at another airline with your current airline employer logo prominently displayed on your social media account.

Pay it Forward

OK, it's time. Cherish your accomplishment; you earned it! If you're confident this is your "forever airline", it's OK to perform the cliché changing of your Facebook profile picture to the tail flash or company logo of your new airline (you know you want to!). Go out and celebrate with your family. You just started the next chapter of the rest of your lives. It's an amazing industry that will provide tremendous benefits for you and your family and allow you to travel the world. In fact, I finished this book while flying home first-class nonrevenue from the French Riviera with my wife. (Remember that ZED fare thing I mentioned in chapter 4? You just have to pay the taxes.)

Yes, you will be on the road a lot, but when you're home, you are 100 percent home. No more going in on your time off to catch up on e-mails or write evaluations. No more deployments, no more time-sucking squares to fill (PME, master's degrees, etc.). Your new office has a window view that even the CEO of any Fortune 100 company can't compare with.

While you celebrate, take a moment to look back on your transition from military to airline pilot. You worked hard for this moment, and you learned a lot along the way. For many of you, this was the first time you ever had to write a résumé, put on a business suit, and interview for a job in your adult life. For some of you, the stars may have aligned perfectly, and your transition went seamlessly from military to airline pilot. Others may have had a rougher time in transition, and maybe it took a little longer to find your new career.

Debrief your personal career transition just as you would as a professional military aviator. How did it go? Did you achieve your transition objectives? If not, why not? Was your game plan valid? Did you execute your game plan properly? What lessons did you learn along the way? If you had to do it again, what would you do differently?

Now I'm going to ask you to pay it forward. We are all brothers and sisters in the profession of arms, a unique fraternity from whom much is expected. We were trained to hold ourselves to a higher standard both in the air and in our conduct as military officers. We owe it to each other to help each other and future generations of military aviators to ensure they benefit from the lessons we learned in transition from cockpit to cockpit.

One of the best ways you can help someone get hired at your airline (or even another airline) is to write recommendation letters. If someone asks you to write a recommendation letter, you should be honored. Don't blow off the request (assuming he or she is a good person whom you would want working at your company...if not, then tactfully tell the person why you don't feel comfortable writing him or her a letter). Spend some time making each letter unique, and make sure you discuss both the person's flying abilities and his or her personal character to the best of your ability. Somebody did the same for you to get you hired; now it's your turn to repay the favor.

Be an informal recruiter for your airline. If you have friends or coworkers who show a strong interest in your airline and you live near the company headquarters, consider arranging a tour for them. Show them around; get them excited about working for XYZ airlines. Make sure your tour just happens to stop by the pilot-hiring department and chief pilot's office to make some introductions. If you don't live near the company headquarters, you can still help your friends out by handing a copy of their résumé into the chief pilot's office and/or the pilot-hiring department.

You can also volunteer to be a formal recruiter. Remember those job fairs you attended for a chance to spend three to five minutes chatting with a recruiter from your airline? You can volunteer to be one of those recruiters. Some airlines will even pay you to do so. As the major airlines transition away from job fairs towards in-house pilot recruiting events, you might consider volunteering to be on the pilot hiring interview team. Being an informal or formal recruiter is not only good for your friends; it's also good for the company. You have a vested interest in selecting the best talent for your airline. After all, these are the pilots you're going to be flying with for the next decade or three.

Another way to pay it forward is to recommend this book and associated website to any military pilot you know who may be thinking about becoming an airline pilot. *Cockpit to Cockpit* is a great gift for both newly winged military pilots and those about to make the transition to civilian life (or partial civilian life in the case of you Guard and Reserve pilots). As you have seen firsthand, knowledge is power. If you found this book helpful, recommend it to a friend, coworker, or family member. Send them the link to the *Cockpit to Cockpit* website www.cockpit2cockpit.com.

Now I'm going to ask you a huge personal favor. I would be extremely grateful to you if you would take just a few minutes to leave a book review on www.cockpit2cockpit.com/reviews. If you're anything like me, you like to be an informed consumer. I always read the reviews before I buy a product online. Please help others who may be on the fence about buying this book to let them know if you think it could help them also. Thanks!

Summary

Thank you for sticking with me through the whole book. I feel like we have created a special bond over the past ten chapters, don't you? Now that we're friends, it would mean a lot to me if you would keep me informed on your progress. Please use the "Contact Us" link of the *Cockpit to Cockpit* website www.cockpit2cockpit.com to provide feedback on the results of your interviews. If you think this book was helpful in your journey, I would love to hear about it. Conversely, if you think there were any areas where I steered you wrong, let me know that also.

You can also help me by acting as my eyes and ears in the transition process. Airlines often change their application requirements, interview process, and so on. If you found any information in this book that is no longer valid or needs updating, please let me know. You can use the "Contact Us" link on the *Cockpit to Cockpit* website to submit your suggestions.

Well, that's it, my friends. Enjoy the ride and stay proficient. As a professional military-trained aviator, you owe it to the flying public to maintain a high degree of knowledge and proficiency. I wish you (and your passengers) smooth air and blue skies.

PS: Don't fuck up the landing!

The Checklist

- **If you are considering changing airlines, don't invest in a 401K at your current airline until you research the rules about becoming vested.**

- **Don't advertise your CJO on social media until you have a confirmed training date with your "forever" airline of choice.**

- **Pay it forward to help other friends/coworkers get hired.**

- **Write letters of recommendation for friends and coworkers who would be good pilots for your new airline.**

- **Help friends and coworkers get hired by hand walking their résumés to the chief pilot and HR department.**

- **Volunteer to work recruiting events with your airline.**

- **Please do a book review for *Cockpit to Cockpit* (in my best Arnold Schwarzenegger voice)..."DO IT NOW!"**

- **Don't fuck up the landing!**

List of Acronyms

AC	Aircraft Commander
AFPC	Air Force Personnel Center
AIS	Advanced Instrument School
ALO	Air Liaison Officer
AMEL	Airplane Multi-Engine Land
AMES	Airplane Multi-Engine Sea
ASES	Airplane Single-Engine Sea
ATP	Airline Transport Pilot
CFI	Certified Flight Instructor
CFII	Certified Flight Instructor Instrument Airplane
CFR	Code of Federal Regulations
CJO	Conditional Job Offer
CRM	Cockpit Resource Management

DO	Director of Operations
EP	Evaluator Pilot
FAA	Federal Aviation Administration
FAPA	Future & Active Pilot Advisors
FECOC	Fighter Electronic Combat Officer Course
FEF	Flight Evaluation Folder
FO	First Officer
GA	General Aviation
HHQ	Higher Headquarters
HR	Human Resources
IMC	Instrument Meteorological Conditions
IFE	In-Flight Emergency
IP	Instructor Pilot
IRC	Instrument Refresher Course
LOI	Line-Oriented Interview
LORs	Letters of Recommendation
MCT	Military Competency Test

MEI	Multi-Engine Instructor
NATOPS	Naval Air Training & Operating Procedures Standardization
NVG	Night-Vision Goggles
OFA	Organizational Fit Assessment
OPR	Officer Performance Report
PCS	Permanent Change of Station
PIC	Pilot in Command
PME	Professional Military Education
PRF	Promotion Recommendation Form
ROE	Rules of Engagement
ROP	(1) Record of Performance (2) Radio Operators Permit
SIC	Second-in-Command
SOF	Supervisor of Flying
Stan/Eval	Standardization & Evaluation
TAD	Temporary Additional Duty
TBNT	Thanks but No Thanks

TDY	Temporary Duty
TMAAT	Tell Me about a Time
TPN	The Pilot Network
UPT	Undergraduate Pilot Training
VFR	Visual Flight Rules
VMC	Visual Meteorological Conditions
XO	Executive Officer

About the Author

Lt Col Marc Himelhoch, USAF (Ret) is a pilot with over 6000 hours total flight time. He grew up in Clearwater, Florida where he met his wife Missy. Marc graduated from Embry-Riddle Aeronautical University in Daytona Beach, Florida with honors and a master of science degree in aeronautical science. In 1995, Marc was commissioned into the USAF as a second lieutenant.

During his air force career, Lt Col (Ret) Marc Himelhoch served as an F-16 instructor pilot (IP) and evaluator pilot. He served four assignments in the F-16 as well as two assignments as an IP in the Euro-NATO Joint Jet Pilot Training program located at Sheppard Air Force Base in Wichita Falls, Texas where he taught primary pilot training in the T-37 and in the T-6A. He has almost 300 combat flight hours and has participated in Operations SOUTHERN WATCH, NORTHERN WATCH, JOINT GUARDIAN, NOBLE EAGLE and IRAQI FREEDOM.

Marc retired from active duty as a lieutenant colonel in 2014. After his retirement he obtained his multi-engine instructor certificate and a B-737 type rating. During his transition from military to airline pilot, Marc interviewed with and received conditional job offers from XOJET, Delta Air Lines, JetBlue Airways, and Southwest Airlines. He accepted an offer from JetBlue and briefly worked there, obtaining an A320 type rating, before being hired by and transitioning to his "final destination" as a pilot with Southwest Airlines. Marc is domiciled in Dallas, Texas where he lives with his wife Missy Shorey who is founder and CEO of Shorey Public Relations.